Flyfishing

ALASKA

• REVISED EDITION •

Anthony J. Route

Johnson Books : Boulder

Spring Creek Press: Estes Park

Dedication

To my parents, Rodney and Elaine

Revised Edition
9 8 7 6 5 4 3 2

Cover design: Bob Schram/Bookends
Cover photograph, silver salmon fishing on Kenai River:
    Alaska Wildland Adventures
Cover photograph, king salmon: Anthony J. Route
Photographs not otherwise credited are by the author
Illustrations by Marcella Hackbardt

Library of Congress Cataloging-in-Publication Data

Route, Anthony J.
  Flyfishing Alaska / Anthony J. Route. — Rev. ed.
      p.   cm.
  Includes bibliographical references (p.   ) and index.
  ISBN 1-55566-150-5 (pbk. : alk. paper)
  1. Fly fishing—Alaska.   I. Title.
  SH467.R65   1995   95-250
  799.1'2—dc20   CIP

Printed in the United States of America by
Johnson Printing
1880 South 57th Court
Boulder, Colorado 80301

Contents

Foreword

There is no doubt whatsoever that fishing in Alaska is one of the great experiences a flyfisher can have. The country and the fish are exceptional, so exceptional that all flyfishers should try to sample them at least once, if not repeatedly.

When I was growing up in Alaska during the 1950s and 60s, much was still unknown about flyfishing for all of the different species there. Rainbow trout and grayling posed no problems, especially in waters where salmon were absent. It was usually a fairly simple, straightforward approach to cast a dry Royal Coachman or Black Gnat and set the hook as the rainbow or grayling rose to intercept the fly. Many of us believed that to catch salmon, however, one had to employ the use of salmon eggs or spinners. Those beliefs were brought about by the fact that we failed to understand the fish we were trying to catch and the ways in which we could use our fly gear.

Flyfishing has changed drastically in the past 30 years. New rod-making materials, fly lines, and fly tying materials have contributed to more successful fishing. With new fast-sinking lines and flies tied of modern synthetic materials, even king salmon can be taken consistently with fly gear. The increased number of creative fly anglers has also added to the information bank of ways and techniques to take all of the species in Alaska.

Tony Route's experience flyfishing for all of the various fish in Alaska, coupled with his skills as a writer and photographer, make him unconditionally qualified to write a book about flyfishing in Alaska. His extensive background as a biologist, guide, commercial fly tier, and in retail tackle sales has provided him with the knowledge to relate the information needed to help you fish in Alaska more successfully. The information contained in this book will help the first-time flyfisher in Alaska approach the experience much better prepared and ready to meet the conditions.

In August of 1986 my wife, Joyce, and I were in Alaska to visit a newly-opened lodge and to spend some time with my family in Anchorage. Tony invited us to go with him to fish a small Kenai Lake tributary for Dolly Varden. Fishing was outstanding, but without his guidance we would never have caught on to the technique necessary for enjoying those scrappy char. The information in this book will give you the knowledge to fully enjoy your Alaska flyfishing.

Marty Sherman, editor, *Flyfishing* magazine
August 28, 1988
Roads End, Oregon

Preface

I was introduced to Tony Route at an Anchorage fly shop where he was employed for a time in 1986. As I remember, I bought some small item that I probably didn't need and left with that certain feeling that one only occasionally has about another human being—here is a man I want to see more of and know better. I wanted another meeting because I left the store with more than a spool of tying thread. Tony had offered me useful advice in a pleasant, unassuming manner that made me eager to learn more from him. And, I wanted to go fishing with him. That chance didn't occur until 1987 when Tony invited me on a February trip to the upper Kenai River to flyfish for a late run of silver salmon and the attendant Dolly Varden that eat the cohos' eggs. In my log book I recorded that fishing was unexceptional that day; Tony caught and released three Dolly Varden and a friend and I were fishless. Unrecorded was my increasing awareness that Tony knew a lot about fish and flyfishing.

The Alaska Flyfishers is a club with over 400 members, affiliated with the Federation of Flyfishers. As a member of the Alaska club's executive board, I asked Tony if he would deliver a presentation at our April 1987 meeting on the Talachulitna River fisheries, an internationally famous flyfishing-only stream. It was a time of controversy because of a proposal by an outfitter to locate a temporary fishing camp and large numbers of anglers on the river. Tony helped us all appreciate the river environs, the salmon, rainbow trout, and grayling fisheries, and potential threats to the "Tal." We left the meeting with a new appreciation and understanding of the river, even those of us who had fished it many times before. Again, there was his knowing advice for us on stream ecology and fish behavior, fishing techniques and equipment, fly patterns, and even rafting tips that were offered out Tony's genuine concern for someone else's safety. That's the way he is, always.

Tony has since addressed the Alaska Flyfishers with stimulating and thoughtful presentations on saltwater fly-fishing and flyfishing stillwater in Alaska. Those of us who have heard Tony or read his many published articles on fly-fishing will tell you he doesn't just specialize in stream fishing for rainbow trout, although he surely is adept at catching this most sought-after Alaska trophy. Tony pursues and catches them all—king, sockeye, pink, chum, and silver salmon, steelhead, cutthroat, and lake trout, Dolly Varden/Arctic char, Arctic grayling, northern pike, and sheefish—with a fly rod. He writes about these topics and these fishes in *Flyfishing Alaska* from his experiences afield on the streams, lakes, and oceans of Alaska and at his tying bench. You may not have the opportunity to fish with Tony, as I have, but in this important volume he will head you to good fishing holes, fundamental flyfishing techniques for Alaska species, and fly patterns that work. The book's title is truly indicative of its contents—a source book of flyfishing opportunities in Alaska. All of it!

Dirk V. Derksen
President, Alaska Flyfishers
November 1988

Acknowledgments

There are so many people that I would like to thank. I could go on for pages listing their names, but it concerns me that I would miss some. This is inevitable because there are many names that I never knew. There have been innumerable brief encounters in fly shops and on the stream, not only in Alaska but everywhere that I have traveled, where flies and information—not names—were exchanged. Like any flyfisher who truly enjoys the sport, I try to learn something from everyone that I meet. So, to all the flyfishers whom I have met, shared information with, and exchanged flies with, thank you.

But as I pursue the itinerant ways of a fanatical flyfisher, one person, my wife Ann, deserves a lot of credit and heartfelt thanks for all the support that she has given me.

ALASKA MARY ANN

Chapter 1
Flyfishing Alaska

Alaska is a big state. It is larger than one-fifth of the rest of the United States, and within its boundaries are spruce forests, tundra, 17 of the 20 highest mountain peaks in the United States, temperate rain forests, villages, small towns, and metropolitan areas. To characterize it in one word, one sentence, one paragraph, or even in one book is a task that would likely fall short of its goal.

To find a common denominator in this land of dramatic differences is an equally difficult task. Flyfishers have water as their common bond, and this may seem to simplify things quite a bit. In reality it doesn't, because Alaska's waters exhibit a variety just as extreme as its other geographic features. Waters of every type, from small streams to large lakes to saltwater bays, dot Alaska's landscape in such numbers that the most avid flyfisher would need an entire lifetime to sample even a portion of them.

The fish encountered in Alaska show just as much diversity as the waters and their surrounding environments. A flyfisher's day could be spent straining to control the underwater gyrations of a lake trout, watching the aerial leaps of a silver salmon, or casting a fly into a thick school of tidewater pink salmon. These species, and many others, are found in the state's waters and may be played against the backdrop of rugged mountain peaks, a forested river valley, or the stark landscape of the open tundra.

If the vastness and variety of Alaska's geography, its waters, and its fish lack common denominators, there remains a common bond in those who visit the state to flyfish. For them, Alaska is a place of great expectations. It is a flyfishing destination that is written about frequently, and readers are often led to believe that every puddle of water in Alaska is teeming with finned behemoths whose only purpose in life is to savagely attack an artificial fly. Writers may make it seem that game trails are more common than human footpaths and that the only signs of other people will be a trapper's derelict cabin or the occasional buzz of an airplane overhead.

There are times when these descriptions are accurate, but it takes more than casual planning to be in such a place at the right time to catch the fish you're seeking.

This book will help you to do just that—be in the right place at the right time.

For each species of fish covered in this book, there is a range map that shows the distribution of that fish throughout Alaska. Also, within the text of each chapter, I mention regions, watersheds, and sometimes specific bodies of water that have particularly good fishing for that species. For the most part, I intentionally try to use broad terms like regions and watersheds as opposed to singling out specific rivers and lakes.

I do this with good reason. For one thing, Alaska is a huge state, and I couldn't possibly name all of the potential places to fish. Secondly, the ones that I do mention stand the chance of having the fishing pressure increase to the point where it might adversely affect the quality of the fishing, and I don't want to be responsible for that. There is no way completely around it though, and throughout the book I'll mention specific places. However, I've been careful to select places that I feel can withstand added fishing pressure or places that are not considered sensitive by myself and my fellow Alaskan flyfishers. When appropriate I will specifically mention some small streams that are listed in Alaska's fishing regulations as fly-fishing-only waters. These places may not be well-known to the visiting angler, but they are far from secret since they're listed every season in Alaska's fishing regulation booklet. I mention them because you, as a reader, deserve to know where you can fish and not have to worry about the pool below you being dredged with treble-hook-laden, half-ounce spoons or skeins of salmon roe.

Planning an Alaskan Trip

How to spend a week or two in Alaska is the major concern of flyfishers once they have decided to go. Should you stay at a lodge? Is it possible to drive around and use the road system as a jumping off point to do some fishing? How about a float trip? Obviously, individual preference and budget constraints will play a big part in deciding which is right for you. It is difficult, though, to make an informed decision without being aware of all your options. With this in mind, let's take a look at what is available.

The most well-publicized type of Alaskan fishing vacation is a stay at a remote lodge. In addition to the fishing, these lodges offer accommodations that range from rustic to elegant. If you are interested in extras that include Jacuzzis, saunas, maid service, and fine dining after a day's fishing, you'll find them among some of Alaska's lodges.

For the sake of comparison, lodges can be grouped together according to the frequency with which they fly clients to fishing spots. Some are called full fly-out or daily fly-out lodges. These lodges do just what their name implies. Each morning anglers board an airplane and fly to the waters they're going to fish. Partial fly-out lodges offer this service on only a specified number of days. For example, during a six-day stay you may fly out on three days and fish the other three days via boat or on foot in the vicinity of the lodge. Lodges that don't offer fly-out services, although you may have to fly to get to them, do not fly you to fishing destinations once you've arrived. Instead, all of the fishing is done via boat or on foot.

How do you decide which is right for you? The amount of money that you can afford to spend is often a limiting factor.

Fly-out fishing in Alaska.

Some lodges cost well over $4,000 per angler per week, and that doesn't include airfare to Alaska. You may simply have to rule out a trip that you cannot afford.

Once you've decided how much you're willing to spend, the decision process can be simplified by preparing a set of questions to ask every prospective outfit. Begin by asking how long they have been in business and how long they have operated under the current management. If an outfit has been in business for a long time with the same management, it's a good indication that they're doing something right. Bad reports travel fast, and it's tough to stay in business if you're not pleasing your customers. However, just because a particular operation hasn't been around for years doesn't mean that it's a bad prospect. A well-run fishing operation can start up anywhere at any time. In the same vein, ask what their percentage of repeat customers is; a high percentage of repeats is a good sign.

Does the lodge cater just to flyfishers? If they have both spin and flyfishers, do they separate them? There is nothing wrong with spin fishing, but different methods require different tactics and techniques, and sometimes they don't mesh. I would rather not give that situation an opportunity to present itself. No one wants to show up for a week of flyfishing only to find that the preferred method of fishing is back trolling in a large river with three people in the boat.

Ask if the manager and guides are flyfishers. Most flyfishers will try their luck in almost any kind of water, but some spots are more suitable than others. If the staff doesn't understand the nuances of flyfishing, you might be fishing less than optimal waters for your entire stay. Furthermore, if the guides don't flyfish, it will be very difficult for them to assess your fly assortment and recommend appropriate local patterns. There will also be little chance of finding fly tying tools or materials on the premises should you run out of a hot pattern.

Inquire about the guides' credentials. Can they tie flies? How many seasons of guiding experience do they have? Remember, these are the people who will be with you on the stream all day.

How many different rivers can you fish in one week? In this case, more isn't necessarily better, but it is nice to see a variety of waters. Some flyfishers like to visit the same stretch of water more than once. They enjoy fishing known water. If that is your preference, ask if it can be arranged.

Ask about the fishing right at the lodge. This is very important, even for fly-out lodges, because there might be a day or two when bad weather prevents flying. If you can't get to some fishing without an airplane, you could spend a lot of time playing cards or tying flies.

How many guests does the lodge handle at one time? Whatever the number, make sure that they have an appropriate number of guides, planes, or boats to accommodate all of the guests. If they are a fly-out operation that handles 20 guests and they only have two planes, each with a capacity of four anglers, you know someone is going to be left standing somewhere. Even so, some lodges are situated very close to prime fishing grounds and are able to make a several trips with a plane or boat every morning to get anglers on the water with little time wasted. This might be the case if their transportation services seem to be less than adequate for the number of clients they handle.

Ask them about their typical day. At what time can you expect to leave the lodge in the morning? How long does it normally take for you to get where you'll be fishing? When do you return? And, will there be any fishing available in the evening after dinner?

The best way to evaluate the experience, dedication, and overall quality of the staff is by talking to people who have previously visited the lodge. References who speak highly of the lodge indicate that you're heading in the right direction. If you know someone who has been to the lodge, they'll be your most important reference for a couple of reasons. If you're both familiar with the other's fishing ability, answers to questions and comments about the fishing are more meaningful. Secondly, a personal friend shouldn't have any reason to make false or exaggerated claims.

However, in most cases, you will not have the luxury of knowing someone who has been to the place you intend to go. In this instance, you will have to query the lodge directly for a list of references. This is a widely-accepted practice, but it's not without its flaws. First of all, there is a good chance that all of the people on the reference list are individuals who thoroughly enjoyed their stay. What business would give out names of people who had not been satisfied with their services? Secondly, since you don't know the people, it may be difficult to determine what they consider a good time. Qualifying the reference person is just as important as the questions asked regarding the destination.

For example, you may discuss the lodge with a person who spends a lot of time business traveling, but who may have little time to fish. He may only fish a couple of days a year. Another person you talk to may fish 100 days a year, all over the country or all over the world. You can never be absolutely sure, but there's a good chance that there is a big difference between what these two people call good fishing.

I think that it's logical to put more weight on the latter's evaluation of the fishing than the former's. But this doesn't mean that the first person's evaluation is of no value. Any veteran traveler gets to know his way around hotels, motels, and restaurants—ask him about the food, the accommodations, and how courteous and helpful the staff were. People who travel because of work are quick to note the creature comforts that make them feel more at home. Of course, the amenities at the lodge do not directly affect the fishing, but if you weren't concerned with them, you probably wouldn't be shopping for a lodge that offers these extras.

Lodges are not everyone's choice for an Alaskan trip. Instead, many flyfishers choose to stay at a tent camp. Now I know that when many people hear the word tent, they have memories of leaky little pup tents erected in their backyards. As a result, there are some people who do not even consider tent camp operations in Alaska. This is unfortunate because there are several excellent outfits in Alaska that use tents. One look at some of the premier tent camps will quickly dispel any doubts you may have about being wet, cold, and sleeping on the ground. The best tent camps have wooden flooring, comfortable bunks, shower facilities, and great food. Ask to see pictures of the camp—you might be surprised at how nice they are.

Typically these camps are set up along rivers at strategic locations so that anglers can either walk to the fishing or go upstream or downstream by boat. Some even offer fly-out fishing. Understandably, tent camps cost less than lodges, and from the standpoint of fishing quality and affordability, a tent camp operation can often be a great bargain.

Float trips are touted by many as the greatest way to experience Alaska's wilderness. There is something special about floating a river and spending some time getting to know it but

Floating Alaskan rivers.

still not having any idea of what the water around the next bend will bring. Of course, without any knowledge at all about what is around the next bend, you had better have a guide with you. Otherwise you stand the chance of floating some nasty whitewater that you should have portaged around.

There are many reputable float trip operators in Alaska, and if you haven't done a lot of floating, it would be a good idea to employ their services. If you do have some river floating experience and you feel comfortable about depending solely upon yourself and your fishing companions, there is no reason you can't do it yourself. Keep in mind that many rivers are a long way from anywhere, and you will have to take care of all your own logistics, from deciding upon where and when to put-in and take-out, right down to your daily meal plan. You may see signs of other people, whether it's meeting another float group or just a floatplane zipping overhead, but don't count on them being there if you need them. Even a minor problem can develop into a major problem when you are miles from nowhere. Be prepared to take care of yourself. If you haven't done this sort of thing before, Alaska may not be the best place to start.

Many of the same questions that are used to query a lodge can be directed at tent camp and float trip operators. Obviously some of the questions will be irrelevant, and others may need to be changed to fit the situation. Here again, references from people who have used the services are very important.

A year in advance is not too early to begin making plans for your Alaskan fishing trip. Addresses for your initial contacts with lodges and outfitters can be gleaned from the pages of many fishing periodicals. Travel agents and booking agents that specialize in fishing and other outdoor-related trips will also be able to give you some information. Many major metropolitan areas throughout the country have sport and travel shows that, depending upon the area in which you live, may have some Alaskan outfits represented. This provides an excellent opportunity to question directly the people involved and to do some comparison shopping. Regardless of how you find out about the prospective places, it's important to keep asking questions until you feel comfortable about how they operate. Communicate clearly, because any misunderstandings can lead to false expectations.

Roadside fishing.

Fishing Along the Road System

Fishing along the road system can be such a markedly different situation than what most people perceive as the ultimate Alaskan wilderness fishing experience that it needs some explanation.

Fishing along the road system is the least costly and easiest way to fish in Alaska. You'll see some great scenery and wildlife, but unless you luck out or happen to be under the tutelage of a knowledgeable resident angler, you'll most likely be sharing your fishing spot with lots of other anglers. Don't get me wrong, I don't want it to sound like there isn't any good road-accessible fishing, because there is, but it is not great by Alaska standards. Does that mean that you can't have a good fishing experience using only the road as your conduit to Alaska's waterways? Absolutely not. You just have to lower your expectations a bit.

Roadside streams, especially once the salmon have arrived, can be as crowded as any urban fishery in the Lower Forty-eight. If you enjoy fishing as a largely social-type of event, you'll have no trouble finding happiness along Alaska's roads. If you're looking for a little more solitude, you'll have to have a lot of savvy and determination. You'll be off to a good start if you can strap on a pack and do some walking.

If you haven't already guessed it, the glory species—like king salmon—tend to draw a crowd. When kings are in waters that are intersected by a road, expect to see a lot more people than fish. There are times when Susitna River tributaries in the Mat-Su Valley and streams on the lower Kenai Peninsula are so crowded with anglers intent on hooking a king that it's impossible to find a place to park your car.

What do you do? Well, if you really have your heart set on a king salmon, muscle your way into the crowd and prepare to use every shred of tolerance you have for the foibles of your fellow man. It's carnival-like and often very entertaining, and I'm always impressed with the number of people who are truly happy and enjoy fishing under such conditions. I, however, prefer to take in the scene from a distance and then slip away to a trout-filled lake.

Speaking of lakes, the lakes of the Matanuska-Susitna Valley are undoubtedly one of Alaska's best kept flyfishing secrets. Not only are they in close proximity to roads, but there are enough of them so that you could fish a different one every day of the summer. There are other lakes, too. The Kenai Peninsula has its share of them, and then there's places like Lake Louise off the Glenn Highway and dozens of lakes along the Denali Highway. Without ever venturing too far from the road you could cast your fly to stillwater rainbow trout, pike, lake trout, grayling, Dolly Varden, and kokanee.

Of course there's stream fishing, too. Streams do attract more attention than lakes, but remember the salmon scenario. Where there are salmon—regardless of what species—there will be crowds. So, hit the salmon streams before the salmon arrive or after the run has peaked and most of the meat anglers have filled their coolers and gone home. Admittedly it is tougher to find a lonely stream than a lonely lake along Alaska's road system, but it's not impossible.

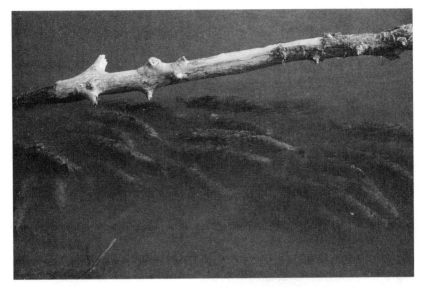

Glacial water and sockeye salmon.

Fishing Glacial Water

Because visitors to Alaska are often unfamiliar with glacial run-off water and frequently have misconceptions about fishing it, it's worth taking a moment to talk specifically about the grayish-green water carrying fine silt from glaciers.

For many visiting flyfishers, the first look at the seemingly opaque water of a glacially-colored river brings disappointment. They think the river is blown out, unfishable. Nothing could be further from the truth. Although the level of turbidity and color are not static and do change, the condition occurs year around, and the fish—and the anglers who pursue them—have learned to live with it.

Obviously, visibility decreases in glacially-tinted water, and it would be illogical to say that fish can see just as well in glacial water as they can in water that is clear. I can tell you that when they want to, fish in glacial streams have no difficulty finding a size 16 nymph or the speck of color associated with a tiny single-egg fly. I've even watched as grayling dimpled the surface of glacial water to feed on floating insects.

Most of the time, however, it's a good idea to use larger patterns when fishing glacial water. A Two-Egg Sperm Fly, for instance, may get more response from the fish than a single-egg fly. Although you might not expect it, dark colors show up much better than light colors. A size 2 Black Woolhead Sculpin or a Purple Woolly Bugger will often get the attention of fish regardless of how glacially-silted the water is. Flies that have sharply contrasting colors, such as chartreuse and black, also work very well.

When fishing glacial waters, many flyfishers employ a method called the attractor-yarn technique, with great results. An orange or other brightly-colored piece of yarn is tied to the leader about two feet ahead of a more somber offering, such as a nymph. The yarn shouldn't float like a strike indicator but instead should sink. Fish are attracted to the bright yarn and then see the fly and take it.

This practice of adding a bit of colored yarn to the leader is thought by many flyfishers to be a necessity when fishing the grayish-green, glacially-silted waters of Alaska. I don't completely agree. I do agree that there are times when the attractor-yarn technique increases the number of hook-ups, but I don't think it's absolutely necessary to use it to catch fish from glacial waters. I've caught plenty of char, trout, grayling, and salmon from glacial water without yarn added to the leader.

As a word of warning, it pays to be cautious when you're wading in glacially-silted water and you cannot clearly see the bottom. Shuffle your feet forward rather than taking big steps. Use your leading foot as a probe and don't lift your other foot until your leading foot has been firmly planted on the bottom. Remember, no matter how shallow the water is where you're standing, the next step could put you into water up to your eyeballs. Wade with caution in glacially-silted water.

What to Bring

What should you bring to Alaska? Depending upon the time of year and your specific destination, your needs will vary, but you should bring a minimum of two rods. My standard traveling companions are a nine-foot, five-weight rod and a nine-and-a-half foot, eight-weight rod. I'll add other rods as conditions require, but those two rods make up the base of my collection. A similar combination, such as a five- and a seven-weight or a six- and an eight-weight, would also be quite versatile.

Specific additions to your rod assortment will be based upon the species you plan to target. For instance, if king salmon are on the agenda, you'll want to tote along a ten-weight, and if you are planning on spending a lot of time fishing for grayling, you'll want to consider taking a four-, three-, or even two-weight rod. While I haven't seen too many rods broken while they were actually being fished, I have seen quite a few succumb to doors and errant footsteps. Carrying a spare or two is always a wise idea. You could get lucky and find a suitable replacement, but don't count on it because you'll probably be a long way from a source for anything that breaks.

Rods should, of course, be matched with appropriate reels and lines. Reels with a dependable click drag are adequate in the smaller sizes, but on the larger models a strong, smooth drag system is a welcome feature. Alaska's fish and fishing conditions vary tremendously, and a wide variety of lines is needed to get the best out of each situation. It is not uncommon to use a lead-core shooting head and a floating line on the same day.

Most flyfishers are rather set in their ways about what goes into their vest, but here are two recommendations anyway. First, in addition to your forceps, get a pair of needle-nosed pliers. Forceps are great for removing small flies from small fish, but they don't fare too well when you are trying to remove a 3/0 hook from a king salmon. Pliers get the job done more easily around big fish and big flies.

Second, a hook hone is something that should be a standard piece of equipment in any flyfisher's vest, but I continue to meet lots of flyfishers who don't carry them. Sharp hooks are a must. After you drag a sculpin pattern across the rocks on the bottom of a stream, you will need to touch up the point. And many hooks, just like knives, aren't extremely sharp when they arrive from the factory.

Don't forget your camera. Even if you're not a photographer, you'll want to have a camera in Alaska. The beautiful scenery, the wildlife, and your big fish, all deserve at least a couple of snapshots. Some of the new weather-resistant cameras are easy to use, and they fit neatly into a shirt pocket or your vest. These are ideal to have while fishing in Alaska's sometimes inclement weather.

A small backpack or a daypack is one of my most indispens-able items. I am never without one, whether I'm driving the Denali Highway or flying around the Iliamna area. In it I put rain gear, cameras, film, extra hat and gloves, spare spools, extra reels, insect repellent, and anything else that I think I may need dur-ing the day. I also include a few items that are nonessential to fly-fishing, like a field guide or two, small binoculars, and insect-collecting equipment. The extra weight doesn't bother me, because the more I put in it, the less I have in my vest tug-ging at my shoulders all day long. Once I get where I'm going, the pack gets conveniently placed on the streambank, in the boat, or in the floatplane if it's staying close by. As an added precaution, instead of putting everything directly into the backpack, I put everything into a waterproof bag first. The kind I use is made for river runners, and it fits nicely into the main pouch of my pack.

What to Wear

Alaska is a great place to pursue the fish of your dreams in a setting that may be so pristine that it seems like a dream. Dur-ing all of this excitement, you may not realize how cold and wet you're getting. Toughing it out may be easy to do when you're staring into the water at some monstrous fall rainbows, but it's not a smart thing to do. Hypothermia is something that you never want to experience, especially if you're miles from nowhere in the middle of Alaska. Proper clothing is important not only for your comfort but also for your safety.

First and foremost for the Alaskan flyfisher is top-quality rain gear. Don't skimp here. Buy the best that you can afford and make sure that you test it, especially the seams, before you take it on a trip. Also make sure that you get a size large enough to cover sweaters and other bulky clothes.

Second in importance are your waders. Neoprene waders are the best type to have in Alaska. Not only do they keep you dry, but they keep you warm as well.

Layering the rest of your clothing is the most efficient way to stay warm. Start with long underwear made of polypropylene, and then use either wool or some type of synthetic pile fiber for each additional layer. Not only will this system keep you warm, but it also makes it very easy to peel off a layer or two when the temperature rises. Synthetic bib overalls now being made by several companies are very well suited for Alaska's cold water. With a pair of these underneath your neoprene waders you'll stay toasty warm even on the most blustery days.

Gloves and hats are also an essential part of the Alaskan fly-fisher's wardrobe. Fingerless gloves of wool, synthetic bunting material, or neoprene will definitely be appreciated when the wind starts whipping across the tundra. Hats worn by flyfishers are often as much a character statement as they are utilitarian. Whichever you lean toward, your selection should conform to at least one standard—it should be able to fit underneath the hood of your rain jacket. I like to carry a baseball-type cap to keep the sun's glare and the rain off of my face and a wool hat to wear during cold weather.

Other essential accessories include polarized glasses, insect repellent, and possibly a head net. Polarized glasses are a must to break through the glare of the water to pick out the shapes of salmon and the char or trout that may be holding behind them. Although it may seem like nitpicking, the color of the lenses in your sunglasses is important. Darker lenses, like gray or green, are fine for sunny days, but they perform poorly in low light conditions. Amber-colored lenses are much better suited to the flat light of Alaska's frequently gray, overcast days.

Insect repellent and, for more serious biting bugs, a head net are small items that can make many days in Alaska much more enjoyable. The concentration of biting insects varies throughout the season, and you may not always need a head net or repellent. But you can be assured that if you forget them, you'll wish you had them. If you don't know it already, you should be aware that most insect repellent will react unfavorably with painted finishes and plastics. Keep repellent away from your fly lines, and as a further precaution, double wrap your bottle of bug dope in polyethylene bags whenever you pack it in your vest or backpack.

Packing Your Gear

Packing for your Alaskan trip can be a formidable task unless you're completely organized. On the floor, spread out everything that you intend to take. Critically review each item for its importance and usefulness. The Alaskan bush is no place to be without a needed piece of equipment, nor is it a convenient place to be carrying around excess baggage.

Don't even think about a hard suitcase. Boats and small planes just aren't designed to carry a bunch of large rectangular objects. Their small, irregularly-shaped spaces are more easily filled by

Packing for plane and boat.

something which will conform to their shape—something like a duffel bag. Begin packing once you have a duffel bag or two big enough to cram all of your stuff into. Everyone has their own system of packing, and it's to your advantage to go through a trial run well before you plan to leave. This will enable you to repack if need be and get everything just right.

Bears

From an outsider's perspective, bears are as much a part of fishing in Alaska as are the fish. Rarely does a conversation about fishing in Alaska end before someone asks about bears. Typically their question takes the form of one of two vastly different queries. Are there places I can fish where there aren't any bears? Or, where can I fish where I'll be sure of seeing a bear? The short answers are real easy—no and nowhere.

The entire state of Alaska is bear country, but that doesn't mean you'll be bumping into them at every bend in the stream. I once went on ten-day float trip through a very remote area and never saw a bear. Yet, a couple of years ago a brown bear was shot in midtown Anchorage. The appearance of a bear is about as unpredictable as their behavior.

Should you worry about bears? Yes and no. If you're fishing at a lodge or with a guide, let the burden of the worry fall on them. If you're on your own, keep your eyes and ears open and adhere to the basic rules of traveling in bear country. Make plenty of noise. The last thing you want to do is to surprise a bear. When you do see a bear, give it plenty of leeway. If a bear wants to take over the pool you happen to be fishing, give it to him, regardless of the number and size of the rainbow trout that may be in the water.

I usually steer clear of recommending or not recommending the use of firearms, but the subject comes up enough so that I can't avoid it. First of all, if you can't recite the basic tenets of safe gun handling and operation, don't even think about carrying one. Unless you are fairly skilled in the use of firearms, you stand a good chance of doing nothing but further aggravating a hostile animal. I firmly believe that some cheechako (Alaskan for someone who hasn't spent a winter here) dancing around a stream with a shiny, new, never-been-fired revolver strapped to his or her waist is a far more dangerous animal than any bear.

All in all, remember that the odds are in your favor. Thousands and thousands of people wander around the backcountry of Alaska every summer, and although bears may cause your palms to sweat and your heart to race, very, very few bear encounters ever become anything more than a good scare.

And while I'm at it, remember that there are other animals out there too. Moose, for instance, are a common sight along many rivers and lakes. Although at times they seem docile, moose demand all the respect that you should show any wild animal. Give them lots of leeway.

Conservation Ethics

Before you read on, I'd like to bring up a very important point. Most fish in these cold Alaskan waters do not grow to large proportions very quickly, and the number of anglers who get to increasingly remote areas mounts every year. Their slow growth rate, combined with the sometimes ease with which they can be caught, could spell doom for strong wild stocks unless a catch-and-release ethic is practiced.

Sometimes when fishing a very remote area, it's easy to assume that no harm can be done by killing one fish. But the question of whether to kill shouldn't even deal with harm or depletion of the resource. We are flyfishers in pursuit of sport fish, and by definition sport fish are valued for the sport they give the angler in their capture, not for their value as food.

Aside from eating fish, there are also those who desire to display their catch on the wall. But home decoration is no more intrinsic to sport fishing than is dining. If you want to preserve the memories of a particularly notable fish, it doesn't have to be killed. Instead of a skin mount, why not consider a lifelike fiberglass mount or an attractive photograph framed with a selection of flies? Flyfishers everywhere should promote catch-and-release by example.

Now that I've stated which side of the fence I'm on as far as catch-and-release is concerned, I'd like to comment briefly on another topic—the issue of best and better. Frequently a statement is made to the effect that Alaska has the best fishing in the United States, North America, or even the world. Or, fishing in Alaska is better than fishing at this place or that place.

Is Alaska the best? There is no doubt that Alaska has some fantastic opportunities for fishing, but what do we mean when we say it has the best fishing? Are we talking about the number of fish caught, the size of the fish, the variety of species, or the ruggedness and beauty of the local environs?

Best means different things to different people, and as we all know, a quality fishing experience, just like a bad fishing experience, can occur anywhere. Alaska is no exception. Is stalking the flats for bonefish any better than fishing for Atlantic salmon in Nova Scotia or fishing a Great Lakes tributary for brown trout or fishing a spring creek in Montana? All are great places to fish, especially if you happen to be the one fishing there.

Comparisons are useful to a degree, but let's leave the critical comparisons of best and better to sports where head-to-head competition can decide a winner. Remember that we flyfish to enjoy ourselves, not to win or lose. With that in mind, it's my hope that this book will help you to make your Alaskan flyfishing adventures as enjoyable as possible.

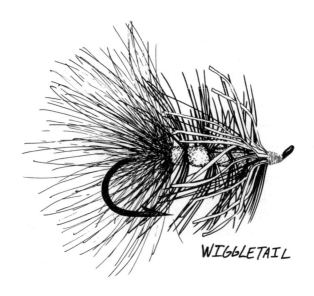

WIGGLETAIL

Chapter 2
King Salmon

Normally I will fish whenever possible, all day long. However, in mid-June the days are awfully long, and as much as I like to fish, I still like to get a few hours of sleep each 24-hour period. At this time of year in south-central Alaska, it really doesn't matter when you sleep, because it's daylight around the clock. Officially the time between sunrise and sunset is about $19\frac{1}{2}$ hours, but you won't find darkness during the other $4\frac{1}{2}$ hours of the day. It's more like an extended period of dusk.

Most of the time I try to sleep during these twilight hours, but on a mid-June float trip for king salmon I decided to do something different. I would try to sleep during the day and then fish through the night.

The fishing during the day had been good, and everyone had caught kings while I alternated between taking photos, grabbing naps, and doing a little fishing. By 10:30 that night everyone else had turned in, but I was just ready to begin. As usual we had chosen a nice bend in the river to camp beside—a bend that had a nice deep slot where kings usually held. I walked down the gravel bar far enough that my backcast would stay clear of the tents and the beached rafts. A salmon porpoised out of the water less than halfway across the stream, and I placed my first cast 10 feet upstream from that spot. The 1/0 Black Boss drifted completely through the lie without being touched. The next 10 minutes yielded the same results.

Then, without warning, my fly hesitated slightly about a third of the way through the drift. Quickly my line tightened up and 25 pounds of king salmon was leaping into the air. A second later my line went slack. My fly line had somehow wrapped around the handle of my reel, and the fish's first surge had easily broken the leader.

Two casts after I had knotted on a new fly, the second king struck. Everything went right this time, and after several jumps and runs I had the fish at the beach. The king weighed about 20 pounds and was just beginning to show the change from bright silver to red.

Hooking these two fish seemed to stir up the action, and for the next couple of hours I hooked and released kings almost continuously. Just before two in the morning, I decided to try out a new series of flies. I had recently been made aware of some new fly tying material that would glow in the dark. This material, called Everglow, and the associated flies, called Everglow Flies, were supposed to be deadly for king salmon. I had tied up a dozen each of several different colors, and I figured this would be a great time to try them. It wasn't really dark—I could still see well enough to tie them on—but it was about as dark as it was going to get.

The results were fantastic. Only occasionally would I have to make more than five casts before I hooked a king. I was still fishing the same pool, and I was amazed at the number of kings in it that were willing to strike a fly. As I released another king, I thought about quitting for the night, but I still had one more color of Everglow Fly to try. The chartreuse-colored Everglow Fly had made a few uneventful drifts through the pool before I felt the line tighten. Instead of immediately racing downstream, this fish moved rather slowly upstream, shaking its head the whole way. The heavy bend in the rod and the slow, methodical head shakes being telegraphed up the line led me to believe it was a large fish.

Once at the head of the pool, the king held for a moment, and then it decided it wanted no part of this tug-of-war contest. The next thing I knew the fish was at the tail of the pool, and it wasn't slowing down at all. The backing flew off my reel, and I knew immediately that I would have to follow this fish if I had any hope of landing it. I splashed on downstream, and while the alder branches brushed against me, I kept up a steady stream of shouts. Early morning on a salmon stream is an excellent place and time to observe wildlife, especially bears. It is rare that they cause any trouble, but I didn't want to surprise one.

After running through a series of three pools, the fish finally thrashed around on the surface and I got my first look at it. It was big—probably 50 pounds or more. It was a bright male with just a touch of pink color beginning to show. I could tell it was tiring, but as I looked around, I realized I didn't have a very good chance of landing it. I was waist deep in water, and the banks were lined with thick alders as far as I could see. With no where to beach it and no one else around with a net, my efforts to remove the fly failed. I stood tangled among the alders as the tippet parted right at the clinch knot.

Three valuable concepts about king salmon fishing were reinforced for me that night: sometimes the most productive time to fish for kings is from 10 P.M. until 2 A.M., Everglow Flies are extremely effective for kings, and it can be very helpful to have someone else standing by with a net or a tailer when you attempt to land a large king salmon.

A salmon tailer, if you're not familiar with one, is a neat little item that allows you to single-handedly lasso a salmon around the base of its tail. Once captured in this manner it is an easy job to control the fish and either remove the hook to release it or quickly dispatch it. They are much more popular in Europe than in this country, and you might not find one sitting on the shelf of your local fly shop. They should, however, be able to order one for you.

In other places king salmon may be called chinook, spring, tyee, or quinnat salmon, but in Alaska they are referred to simply as kings. King. It's an appropriate name for a fish that, in terms of brute strength, is truly the king of Alaska's game fish. Frequently topping the 50-pound mark, king salmon (*Oncorhynchus tshawytscha*) give the flyfisher a rare opportunity to do battle with a very large fish in a freshwater environment.

Male king salmon.

While in the ocean, adult king salmon have a white belly and silvery sides, and they may be dark blue to greenish on top. Normally both the upper and lower lobes of the caudal fin show irregularly-shaped spots, and there are also spots along the back and the dorsal fin. One way to make certain that you have a king is to get a good look at the gums on the lower jaw as you remove your fly. The teeth on a king salmon will emerge from a black gum line. On a silver salmon, which you might confuse with a king if you're new to Pacific salmon, the teeth emerge from a white or gray gum line.

Now you may be thinking that it's rather strange to offer this key to distinguish between a king and a silver salmon. The kings are early spring- and summer-run fish, while normally silvers do not show until much later in the season. When would it be necessary to distinguish between the two? Well, in most freshwater systems it isn't necessary. Any kings that are around will be noticeably larger and in a bright red, post-spawn condition when the earliest of the silver salmon arrive. But if you're casting your fly into the saltwater of southeast Alaska during late summer, you could hook into a fresh silver or a feeder king. Feeder kings are fish that are not yet sexually mature and are present in the

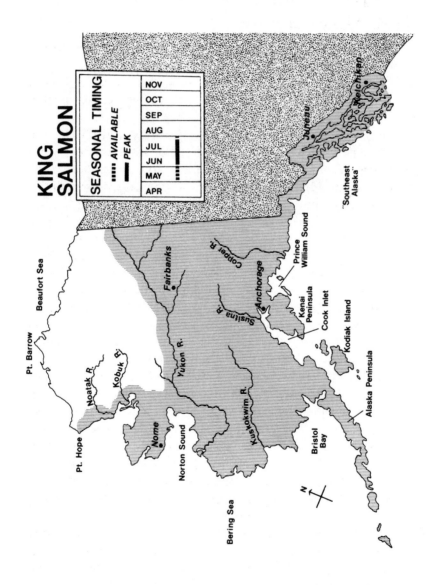

KING SALMON

SEASONAL TIMING

▪▪▪▪ *AVAILABLE*
▬▬ *PEAK*

NOV	
OCT	
SEP	
AUG	
JUL	▮
JUN	▮
MAY	┋
APR	

Southeast's coastal waters throughout most of the year. If you're in the Southeast and you don't know whether you have a king or a silver, just check the gums on the lower jaw.

Kings: Where and When

The range of the king salmon in Alaska stretches from the Southeast northward to Point Hope, and on occasion strays can be found even farther north. As a general rule, runs of kings begin to thin out once you get much farther north than the Yukon River.

One of the most well-known areas for king salmon is Cook Inlet. The Kenai River, which drains into Cook Inlet, receives a lot of attention, and not without good reason. An angler on the Kenai River stands a good chance of hooking into a king salmon of 60 pounds or more. The Alaska state record for king salmon is a 97-pounder that came out of the Kenai River in 1985. Nearly every year there are unsubstantiated reports of even larger fish that got away, and those who make a career out of pursuing king salmon believe that it is only a matter of time before the Kenai River produces a king that weighs more than 100 pounds.

Another reason for its popularity is the fact that the Kenai River is located on Alaska's highway system just three hours south of Anchorage, Alaska's largest city. The Kenai is a wide, deep, glacially-silted river that maintains about a six-mile-per-hour current. As a result, it's not the best place to pursue kings with a fly rod. Many guide services concentrate solely on Kenai River king salmon, but none of them cater specifically to those wanting to try for kings on a fly rod. Although there are flyfishers who do quite well there, a first-time angler on the Kenai could spend a lot of time just finding spots that are suitable for flyfishing. Unless you are teamed up with an angler who fly-fishes and knows the river intimately, the Kenai River is not a best bet for the visiting flyfisher intent on taking kings on the fly.

There are a few enterprising flyfishers who are becoming quite adept at taking Kenai River kings. Shunning traditional big river boat-fishing tactics, they are making their mark from the river bank. The wide, deep river seems to diminish in size when they start rigging up their 12-, 14-, and 16-foot spey rods. With these large, two-handed rods they can throw the fly incredible distances and mend an enormous amount of line. The result is that they can probe holding waters that were previously only accessible to the boating angler.

Some of these long-rod aficionados have even taken to the beaches. The kings that migrate up Cook Inlet often travel fairly close to shore once they approach river mouths, and many times fish can be seen rolling on the surface within reach of the spey rod. This, flyfishing's answer to surf casting, is relatively new in Alaska, and only time will tell how much success it will have. One thing is for sure—an increasing number of spey rods are making appearances during the king season.

Other streams along the road system on the Kenai Peninsula are much better suited, in terms of size, to flyfishing, but during the king run it is common to encounter very crowded conditions on these waters. It is difficult to cast comfortably and to follow a hooked fish when the river banks are lined with anglers. If, however, you're not deterred by crowds, the smaller size and depth of the Kasilof River and the Anchor River offer flyfishers a much better chance of hooking a king salmon. Not on the Kenai Peninsula but still on the road system, the Gulkana River is less crowded than Kenai Peninsula streams and offers flyfishers a decent shot at king salmon, particularly if they float the river.

Any flyfisher is much better off flying out to a less accessible area. Many outfitters and air taxi operators offer short, convenient flights to other places in the Cook Inlet drainage such as the Deshka River, Alexander Creek, and Lake Creek. Here you still will not be alone, but it will be far less crowded than at the roadside spots.

Good to excellent fishing opportunities for kings are found in many places throughout Alaska. The Karluk River on Kodiak Island has a good run of kings, as do many of the waters in the Bristol Bay area. The Nushagak River and its tributaries are home to thousands of king salmon, and the Yukon River system also gets a very healthy return every year. While fishing the mainstem of rivers like the Yukon and Nushagak may not be the best for flyfishers, there are plenty of smaller waters that drain into these rivers that are tailor-made for catching kings on a fly. The Naknek River and the Alagnak River in southwest Alaska don't offer similar tributary-type fishing, but the main stems of these two rivers are popular destinations among flyrodders casting for kings.

Run timing and spawning dates for king salmon, like other salmon in Alaska, are not static, homogeneous events. This is due in part to the wide range in which they are found and in part to the whims of the fish. In southeast Alaska, the months of May and June are prime, while the Cook Inlet area begins to see fish in May, with the best fishing time being from June on into July. Kings will enter the Yukon River in June, and the Bristol Bay area sees fish by mid-June, with the prime fishing weeks being the first and second week of July.

If you fish within these very relative and sometimes variable time periods, you stand a good chance of being able to catch king salmon that are still in good condition. There have even been some reports of kings in good condition being caught well into August. Some of these stories come from very reliable sources, and it has piqued my interest enough for me to plan to do some experimenting in the next few seasons.

The Life Cycle of Kings

Partly responsible for the king's large size is their longevity. Juveniles may remain in freshwater feeding on insects for two, and in some rare cases, three years. Young fish, known as parr, will lose the dark vertical stripes on their sides, commonly called parr marks, as they begin their seaward migration. Now called smolt, they become silvery in color and begin to go through a physiological change which prepares them for life in saltwater. Once in the ocean, their body weight increases rapidly, and on the average they put on as much as one pound per month. As their size increases, they will feed on a variety of different ocean organisms, including shrimp, herring, and squid. The return migration to their natal streams begins in the late winter, and as a result, kings are the first salmon of the year to show up in Alaska's rivers. At this time these returning fish may be anywhere from three to seven years old.

Upon reaching the spawning grounds, the female begins to dig a redd with her powerful tail. The finished redd is usually about four feet long and 15 inches deep. During construction of the redd, a dominant male is usually close by the female, but she pays him little attention and takes time only to drive away other female fish. After finishing the redd, the female is joined by the dominant male, and sometimes a few

Small king from Cook Inlet. Doug Kennemer.

other males, who eject sperm over the eggs she deposits in the bottom of the redd. The female then swims forward, kicking up gravel and debris, which cover the eggs.

Then she begins the process again, continuing until she has deposited all of her eggs. These events may take place over a period of several days, and she may continue to dig in front of the redd for a week or more. Finally she will no longer be able to hold in the current, and she will drift downstream and die. The male may go on to mate with a few more females, but fish of both sexes weaken and eventually death will overtake them. All king salmon, as well as all of the other salmon species in Alaska, die after they spawn.

To the first-time viewer, the sight of salmon carcasses littering the stream bottom and its banks may seem to be a colossal waste, but nature in its intricate way is providing for the young. The rotting fish give the freshwater ecosystem a boost in productivity, and even though the offspring never get to see their parents, they indirectly benefit from their death. When the fry emerge the following spring, the abundant organisms they feed upon are there, in part, because of the adults who fertilized the stream with their bodies the previous season.

Fly Patterns for Kings

When speaking of flies for king salmon, the terms bright and gaudy are understatements. Fluorescent colors are very popular because kings often show a preference for them. Many well-known king flies use fluorescent red, pink, green, yellow, or chartreuse as their predominant color. In staying with the bright and gaudy syndrome, these fluorescent-bodied patterns are frequently supplemented with bright metallic or Mylar tinsels and piping. A third advantageous element to add to any king fly is some material that moves well in the water. Marabou fills the bill quite nicely.

The prototypical king fly is the Wiggletail. Wiggletails are tied in a number of different colors. They have an undulating marabou tail, a chenille body of the same color, and a collar of silver Mylar piping. Fluorescent color, metallic flash, and good movement in the water are each a part of the Wiggletail. Any flyfisher intent on catching kings should have a box with at least a couple of pink, orange, and chartreuse Wiggletails.

Wiggletails are not the only flies that kings will take. There are many flies that do not employ all the components of the Wiggletail but still work quite well. Large Woolly Buggers and Bunny Flies have accounted for many king salmon. Both of these fly types are commonly tied in bright pinks and shades of orange. However, black, purple, and brown, as well as other drab colors, will often take kings, especially on bright days in shallow water situations. The chartreuse Bunny Fly deserves special mention, because it has emerged as a front runner in my assortment of king salmon flies. During the past couple of seasons I have caught kings with it from the Gulkana River to Bristol Bay.

The Flash Fly, which is so popular among silver salmon flyfishers, is also an excellent fly for taking king salmon. In the past, it was the fly of choice when fishing glacially-silted or otherwise discolored water. Although it will catch fish under these conditions, it is not the best fly to use. Under discolored water conditions or when you have to fish very deep, it's becoming very apparent that fluorescent colors produce the most strikes.

Flies tied with glow-in-the-dark material arrived on the Alaskan scene in the mid 1980s, and they have since proven their worth. These Everglow Flies are definitely a top-10 fly pattern for king salmon. The Everglow material is available in a number of colors, but red, orange, and chartreuse are my favorites for kings.

Tarpon-style flies have found their way into Alaska's waters, and they are responsible for taking many kings. Deep Water Whistlers in orange and black and in red and white are very productive. They are especially important to have on hand when the kings are holding deep.

The Alaskabou series of flies are very effective for king salmon. They are tied in a variety of colors and are often laced with Flashabou or Crystal Flash. Orange and purple, cerise and purple, white and pink, and chartreuse and white are the most popular color combinations. It seems that every season on every watershed a new color combination is being touted as the best, so go ahead and experiment with whatever colors appeal to you.

The size of your flies is a personal choice, but there are a few general guidelines to follow. Commercially-tied king salmon flies will range from size 4/0 to size 4, but it isn't necessary to carry patterns in each of these sizes. Do your wallet and your heavy fly vest a favor and choose a sequence where you skip a size. I like to carry sizes 3/0, 1/0, and 2, but many anglers feel more comfortable with sizes 4/0, 2/0, and 1. Choose the sequence of sizes that best coincides with your other tying needs.

Obviously you will want a stout hook for such large fish. There are several good ones on the market, but I usually opt for Mustad #3407. Here my choice isn't based so much on strength as on the fact that most of my king flies find their way into saltwater at one time or another, and I need something that is corrosion resistant.

Once you have assembled this bewildering selection of candy-colored flies, you will have to decide which one to use. A good rule to follow is: as the water becomes deeper or more discolored, use a bigger, brighter fly. Conversely, as the water becomes shallower or clearer, select a smaller, more somber fly. Sounds simple, right? Wrong. This is just a starting point, one that works a fair amount of the time. When this rule breaks down, you are on your own to experiment. The chances are good that you will find a fly that works tremendously well for one hour, one day, or one week. When it stops working, and it probably will, you are back to square one.

Tactics for Kings

The challenge in fishing for kings, and most other salmon in Alaska for that matter, is in finding a fly that elicits an aggravation response, one that will cause the fish to strike, not sulk or swim away in fear. Effective flies change from day to day and week to week, and as a result, each time you fish for kings you may have to go through several different flies before you find what particular type is working the best.

One thing is sure. You will be unsuccessful unless your fly is coming within inches of the fish. Once you can consistently drift your fly right by the kyped jaws of kings, you will be on track. If your first attempts spook the fish, try a smaller, more somber-colored fly. If your larger flies are simply neglected, you are probably not getting your fly close enough to the fish. Some days you will almost have to bump them on the nose.

At times the strike of a king will be extremely violent, and the fish may jump or take off on a torpedo-like run before you even realize what is happening. In this situation, there's nothing to do but hang on to your rod. However, don't always count on such a spectacular strike. Many times a king will simply swing its head to one side, clamp down on the fly, and then quickly spit it out. If you're sight-fishing, it's easy to counter this move by simply tightening up on the line as the king mouths the fly.

If you can't see both the fish and the fly clearly, you will have to rely on a momentary hesitation of line to tell what is happening. When you are blind-fishing discolored water, it is important to get the fly deep. Kings will rarely move up for a fly so keep the fly as close to the bottom as possible. Fishing a deep, dead-drifted fly and being able to detect the strike requires quite a bit of finesse—something not normally associated with king salmon fishing.

By now you have probably surmised that technique is very important if you want to be successful catching king salmon.

You are right. In fact, I'll go out on a limb and say that 90 percent of the time, presentation is more important than the pattern. Being able to select the right line to get a controlled drift at the same depth the fish are holding is the most critical part of your presentation. The best technique employs nothing more than an across-stream or quartered down-and-across-stream cast and then paying close attention while the fly drifts. It's a simple wet-fly swing, no more, no less.

Although the standard wet-fly swing, dead-drift presentation is usually the best, it does sometimes pay off to spice up your drift. Retrieving your fly in foot-long strips as it drifts in front of a group of fish will often bring about vicious strikes. Another tactic that occasionally works is to get directly upstream from holding fish and let the fly drift right into them. Once it has passed behind them, quickly strip the fly forward until it is in front of them again. Many unreceptive kings will belt a fly as it comes up quickly from behind them.

Once you have hooked a king salmon, you will have entered an uncommon realm of flyfishing, that of fighting a very large fish. Most anglers are not fortunate enough to live

Female king salmon.

in or travel frequently to an area where they can consistently catch fish of 30 or 40 pounds. If you fall into this category, don't be surprised if you lose the first couple of kings you hook. It is little different than landing smaller fish with lighter gear, but it is often perceived to be quite a bit more difficult. Perceptions can change your actions, and when 40 pounds of king salmon clears the water, anyone will get excited. It is easy to get so excited that you make a mistake, and you can well imagine that any mistake made will result in a lost fish.

Here are a few other things to keep in mind while fishing for kings. When a king makes its first run, do not try to stop it. Add some drag, but think in terms of controlling the fish, not stopping it. Let the fish work against itself. The more runs and jumps that it makes, the easier it will be to land. Never let a king hold downstream from you for any length of time. This is essentially giving the fish a rest. If possible, move upstream or downstream with the fish so you can exert sideways pressure on it. Positioning yourself and your rod so that you can apply pressure from the side is very important. This will allow you to tire it sooner, and consequently, land the fish faster with as little harm done to it as possible.

Very large fish can be tough to handle once you've brought them close to your side, and a fishing partner can really help out once you get to this stage. A net is a very handy item to have during the final stages of a struggle, but because it has to be so large, it's a real bother to carry one around. For ease of use and economy of size, it is tough to beat a salmon tailer. If you want to or have to do it out of necessity, you can land and release a king by yourself with the aid of a tailer. This is often very difficult to do with a net.

Equipment for Kings

The number of anglers who are flyfishing for king salmon has increased dramatically over the past couple of years. Although there are many anglers who have been catching kings for a long time, a large number of flyfishers have only recently bought or borrowed the tackle needed for kings. Many anglers who fly-fished for other salmon and for trout still pursued kings with only conventional tackle. Some thought that the fly gear needed was too expensive, while others who had unsuccess-fully tried to land kings on their seven-weights, just didn't think it was possible. And, of course, there is the incredulous grin of the neophyte angler who lands a few trout or grayling on his first fly rod and says, "You're kidding, right? You don't really catch kings on fly rods. Do you?"

Because of the sheer size and strength of these fish, you'll need appropriately heavy tackle. A 10-weight is the most widely accepted size of rod to use for king salmon. I don't see any need to go much heavier, but I wouldn't recommend gear that is much lighter. Sure, kings have been caught on much lighter tackle, but it shouldn't be attempted unless you don't mind the possibility of seriously damaging your gear and maybe losing the fish of a lifetime. In the past three years, I've seen a number of name-brand, high-quality, 10-weight rods that were quickly changed from two-piece rods to three-piece rods while doing battle with a king salmon. I was never there to witness the events, and I can't be sure that the rods weren't being mis-handled, but it does illustrate the point of what can happen when you hook into a king.

More than likely you'll hear plenty of wild stories when it comes to king salmon fishing. If you listen closely, you'll find that no one catches a king salmon that weighs any less than 40 pounds. And the second or third time the story is told, the same fish will be much closer to 50 pounds. Even though some of the weights may be exaggerated, it still pays to secure the best gear available.

When considering a rod for king salmon, it's important to choose one that will not only handle the line and the heavy flies, but one that has a lot of backbone. The final minute of battle with a king salmon is very crucial, because once the fish has tired, you will need a rod that has enough muscle to maneuver the fish out of heavy currents where it can be netted or tailed prior to release. It's surprising how much strength is needed to move a fish of such size after it has stopped struggling. This is even more noticeable if you're fishing from a boat and you have to lift a fish to the surface. Anyone who has ever fished for tar-pon or other large saltwater fish knows how difficult this can be.

Your choice of reel is also very important. First of all, it must be able to handle the appropriate line plus 200 yards of back-

Heavy tackle for kings.

ing. Some people prefer to load their reels with 30-pound backing, but I usually stay with 20-pound. The only time I would recommend using backing heavier than 20 pounds is if your leaders are heavier than 20 pounds. If you use a leader tippet of 25 pounds and your backing is only 20 pounds, you run the risk of having your backing break instead of your leader. This could mean not only a lost fish and lost fly but a lost fly line as well.

As for the amount of backing, I don't find it very advantageous to have much more than 200 yards. The chances of landing a king that gets more than 200 yards down river are not too good. Two hundred yards is a long way in any river, and if you can't follow the fish and regain line your chances of landing it are nil.

Because king salmon can grow to such large sizes, only reels that have a dependable drag system are normally used. A smooth, strong drag is, without a doubt, invaluable in landing kings, but many flyfishers, not used to fishing for such large fish, place too much emphasis upon it. Even with reels that have heavy-duty drag systems, I prefer to keep the drag setting relatively light and add additional drag by applying pressure to an exposed rim with my hand. During the course of a fight, I find it much easier to vary the drag this way than by using a mechanism to increase or decrease the drag.

Using my hand on the exposed rim, I can feel exactly how much drag I'm applying and can apply it quickly, and I don't run the risk of cranking down too hard and breaking off the fish. If I use some type of mechanism to vary the drag, I run the risk of adjusting it in the wrong direction—tightening it when I think that I'm loosening it and vice versa. Either mistake could cost you a fish.

King salmon are fished for under a variety of different conditions in Alaska, and the flyfisher who does not carry a wide range of line types will not be able to catch kings as consistently as one who does. There are times when king salmon can be easily spotted and fished for in water depths of four feet and less. Here, a floating line and a leader of the appropriate length to let the fly sink to the level of the fish can be used with great success. This is often the situation encountered once the fish have moved well upstream and are approaching their spawning areas.

In the lower sections of rivers, a sink-tip line is almost always the line of choice. Here it is necessary to have a range of sink-tip lines so that you can fish depths of up to 15 feet or more. Twenty-foot sink-tips or high density, fast-sinking, shooting tapers will outperform other line types in these situations. Shooting heads are preferred by many anglers because they can be changed quickly until you find the one that gets to the correct depth. Also, it is much more economical, in terms of space and money, to carry a wallet full of shooting heads rather than a collection of spare spools for a large and expensive reel.

Leaders for king salmon are a simple matter. With sinking shooting heads and sink-tip lines, all that's needed is a four-foot section of 10- to 18-pound monofilament. Fourteen-pound test is a good all-around size to use, but other factors such as personal preference, the type of water being fished, and the prevailing size of the fish may cause you to go up or down in leader strength accordingly.

Until recently, king salmon had been overlooked by many flyfishers who were intimidated by the size of the fish and the heavy, and sometimes expensive, tackle that is needed to catch them consistently. But now, even casual flyfishers are gearing up for Alaska's king season. The thrill of landing these freshwater giants is unparalleled, and with ever-increasing frequency, flyfishers are coming to Alaska to do battle with one of North America's largest freshwater sport fish—the king salmon.

BRASSIE

Chapter 3
Sockeye Salmon

My first encounter with Pacific salmon was with sockeye salmon. I'd been in Alaska only a couple of months when a fisheries biologist friend of mine hinted, with vague directions, about a small stream that supported a good run of sockeye salmon. Best of all, it was practically never fished. With a topographic map, it didn't take me long to spot three potential streams in the area that he'd discussed.

After leaving one of the Kenai Peninsula's traffic-filled roads, I bushwhacked through the brush for an hour or so. Eventually I stumbled across the first of the three streams that I had outlined on my map. I wasn't sure that I had the right one, but after I put on my Polaroid glasses, I really didn't care. I could see fish all over the place.

Having never seen anyone fish for sockeye salmon, I put on my usual floating line and a nine-foot leader. The fish were holding close to the bottom, but the water in the deepest spots was only about four feet deep. The water was very clear, and I figured a sparsely-tied pattern on a large hook would sink quickly enough to get down to the fish during a drift. Tied sparsely, I also hoped that my fly wouldn't spook the fish.

I don't remember what pattern I tied on first, but I do remember having only two fly boxes with me, one with Atlantic salmon hairwings and another that contained some Michigan steelhead patterns. I guess it doesn't matter what fly I tied on first, because I caught fish all day long, and I used flies from both boxes. Because the conditions seemed perfect to do so, I couldn't resist tying on a dry fly. I tied on a Bomber and alternated it with the various wets that I was using, giving them an hour's worth of fishing time. I caught and released plenty of sockeye salmon, but none rose to the dry fly.

Even though the fish and the fly were clearly visible in the water, I still had to pay very close attention. Most of the takes were very subtle, and the sockeye would quickly spit the fly out. Usually the fly had to come within inches of a sockeye's mouth to get a strike, but on a number of occasions a fish would dart out a foot or more to the left or right to grab it. Not once, though, did a sockeye move up or down in the water column for a fly.

When I told people about this fishing adventure the following week, I was immediately accused of snagging fish. Sockeyes, I was told, don't strike flies. No amount of arguing would change their minds. They firmly believed that sockeye salmon would not hit an artificial fly or lure. To catch them with rod and reel, they had to be foul-hooked. Later I did meet some flyfishers who were fully aware that sockeyes could be taken on flies. They even expressed the notion that there were times when sockeyes would hit just about any fly that was presented properly. They were quick to point out, however, that there are many anglers who feel very strongly that sockeyes will not strike an artificial lure. As a consequence of this belief, foul-hooking these fish is an accepted practice in many areas.

The Kenai Peninsula's Russian River, located about 100 highway miles south of Anchorage, is a flyfishing-only river and is one of the most heavily fished rivers in the

Bright sockeye caught on fly.

state. It is a perfect example of this foul-hooking charade. The Russian River gets two distinct runs of sockeye salmon (or red salmon, as they are sometimes called) every summer, and throngs of people show up to fish for them.

The flyfishing-only aspect of it is not quite what you would expect. Fairly heavy spinning outfits with twenty-pound test lines are the norm. A Coho Fly, which is nothing more than two colors of bucktail attached to a long-shanked hook, is the preferred fly. Eighteen inches ahead of the fly a piece of lead is attached to the leader, and then this creation is lobbed upstream and allowed to drift into holding salmon, literally hitting them on the head. Once the fly reaches the vicinity of the sockeye's mouth, the angler sets the hook. As long as the hook is embedded somewhere in front of the eye, the fish is usually declared legal and added to the stringer. (Snagging in freshwater is illegal in Alaska.)

What you may also find amazing is how successful some people are at snagging fish in the mouth. Very adept individuals can, in a cast or two, adjust their weight and leader so that the final inch or two of their leader will slide right into the open mouth of a holding salmon. A quick tug on the line then drives the barb of the hook into the salmon's mouth—albeit from the outside in. No fish is safe from someone who is an expert with this method, and outside of nets or explosives, it is the surest way of removing a fish from a stream. Although it's not sporting—or technically legal—the agencies who manage the Russian River and post signs proclaiming it a flyfishing-only stream prefer to avoid the issue.

If you're planning to flyfish Alaska and would like to catch some sockeye salmon, don't be surprised if someone tells you that reds don't hit flies. Just smile and say, "Yes, that's what I've been told." And if you happen to be on the Kenai Peninsula when the sockeyes are in, by all means stop at the Russian River (if you can find a place to park) and watch some of the action. There is a sort of carnival-like atmosphere, and you will see a part of Alaska that most people don't even realize exists—elbow-to-elbow angling.

In the ocean, sockeye salmon (*Oncorhynchus nerka*) have bright silvery sides and metallic blue to greenish backs. They lack the black spots that are common to some other species of salmon, and instead have fine black speckling. As spawning time draws near, their bodies turn bright red, and their heads turn dark green. The males go through even further changes and develop hooked jaws and a humped back.

Although their relative abundance varies greatly from place to place, in Alaska they can be found from the Southeast north to the Seward Peninsula on the north side of Norton Sound. The greatest concentration of sockeye salmon is in the Bristol Bay region where tens of millions of fish return annually. The Kvichak, Ugashik, and Nushagak

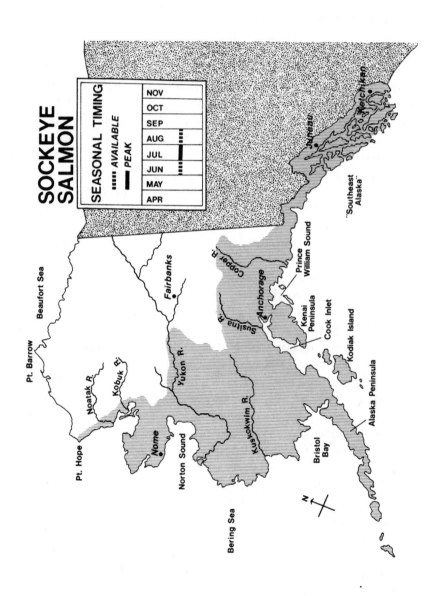

SOCKEYE SALMON

SEASONAL TIMING

▪▪▪▪ AVAILABLE
▬▬ PEAK

NOV	
OCT	
SEP	
AUG	
JUL	
JUN	
MAY	
APR	

River systems are among the biggest producers in the area. The Kvichak River alone, for instance, gets a return of sockeye salmon counted not in the hundreds of thousands but in the millions.

The Life Cycle of Sockeyes

The sockeyes' return to freshwater may occur anytime from June through August. The timing of their specific runs in different watersheds, like their abundance, varies greatly. In some places, such as on the Kenai Peninsula, sockeyes may show up as early as the second week of June. Generally the month of July is considered the peak period to fish for them throughout their range in Alaska.

Spawning usually, but not exclusively, takes place in streams and rivers that are connected to a lake. The time it takes for the eggs to hatch is largely dependent upon the water temperature, and in most cases the fry emerge from the gravel sometime between April and June. Since sockeyes most commonly spawn in streams that have a lake somewhere within their system, the juveniles migrate either upstream or downstream to the lake. How they know whether to go upstream or downstream is not clearly understood, and in a few places they remain in the stream.

For the one or two years that the parr remain in freshwater, they feed on zooplankton and insect larvae. As their stay in freshwater comes to an end, they begin to lose their parr marks and become more silver in color. These smolt now begin their migration to the ocean. This journey to the sea may occur anytime between April and July depending upon their location and the weather conditions for that particular year.

Adult sockeyes return to the stream where their life began after they've spent two or three years in the ocean. As is the case with other salmon, female sockeyes dig three to five redds and deposit anywhere from 2,500 to 4,500 eggs in them. The actual spawning act may be done with a number of different males, and likewise, males may spawn with several different females.

Sockeyes, like most other salmon, get very territorial once they begin to spawn. When they are at this stage, they will

Sockeye salmon.

very likely hit any fly that happens to drift by them. Unfortunately, this isn't when you want to catch them. Bright red and green spawners are usually full of scars and bruises from their long journey, and a good sporting ethic does not include catching fish while they are on their spawning redds. But if you're fishing for other species that are sharing a reach of water with spawning sockeyes, you'll eventually hook one. When you do, it will probably act very lethargic and refuse to move from the vicinity of its redd.

Don't judge them too harshly for this, because when they're bright, they make repeated runs and often jump clear of the water. In fact, there are many anglers who rank the sockeye ahead of the silver salmon in terms of fighting capability. Although silver salmon generally have the better reputation as far as fighting goes, I've caught sockeyes that will run just as far and jump just as often as any silver salmon of similar size.

Fly Patterns for Sockeyes

Most of the flies intended for sockeye salmon are tied too full and are far too large. When the average weight of the fish sought after is around eight pounds, flyfishers naturally reach for fairly large hooks. There is no doubt that a sockeye salmon is capable of inhaling a big fly, but the question remains—do sockeyes prefer a large or a small fly?

Flies for sockeyes are normally tied on a size 4 hook, and flies this size and even larger have accounted for many sockeyes. In most instances, however, I believe that a smaller fly will be more successful. It has been my experience that sockeye salmon are almost always more willing to hit something closer to a size 6, 8, or 10. Even with these smaller flies it's still important to dress them sparsely.

One theory suggesting why sockeyes prefer smaller flies than the other salmon has to do with the food habits of sockeye salmon. As juveniles, sockeye salmon are mainly plankton feeders, while the other species of salmon of the same size and age actively chase and consume much larger prey. For instance, it's not unusual to see juvenile silver or king salmon rising to take insects off the surface of a stream. Likewise, they'll often take a small dry fly or nymph. Juvenile sockeyes, on the other hand, never exhibit this behavior. Even as subadults in the ocean, sockeye salmon regularly eat food items that are much smaller than the herring and other baitfish that make up the diet of other salmon. Perhaps it is this tendency to naturally select smaller food items that makes sockeyes more susceptible to small, sparse flies.

In accordance with this theory, an excellent pattern to use for sockeyes is a sparsely-tied Gold Comet. With a thin ginger tail, flat gold-tinsel body, two turns of ginger hackle, and bead-chain eyes, it's best tied on a size 8 hook. Other Comets in silver, orange, and pink are also frequently successful takers of sockeye salmon. Another fly with bead-chain eyes, the Boss, is also a very effective fly for sockeyes. It can be tied in a number of different colors, but black and chartreuse are the most popular. There are many other typical Alaskan salmon patterns that can be used successfully for sockeyes including the Polar Shrimp, the Sparkle Shrimp, and the Everglow Flies, but remember that they should be tied much more sparsely than patterns typically used for steelhead and other salmon.

Fresh from the ocean.

Good sockeye salmon flies are, in fact, so stylistically different from run-of-the-mill salmon flies, that a whole series of flies has been developed for them, the Sockeye Orange. The original pattern was nothing more than a wing of squirrel hair dyed black and a hot-orange hackle tied on a nickel-plated hook. Nowadays they are tied in a variety of different colors and on different hooks. They all, however, retain the slimness and sparseness of the original.

One of the more unusual salmon flies used for sockeyes is the Montana Brassy, also known as the Brassie. The first Brassies that I ever used were tied on size 18 and 20 hooks. They had a body of fine copper wire and a head and thorax of dubbed fur. They were tied with the intention of imitating small Diptera. Once while fishing in the Iliamna area, I was surprised to hear that the hot fly for sockeye salmon was a Brassie. The first thing I pictured in my mind was one of those midge imitations I'd been introduced to several years ago, but the fly proved to be similar only with respect to the body material. The Brassie used for sockeye salmon has a copper wire body and a sparse wing of either white calf tail or bucktail. This very simple and effective fly is best tied in sizes 6 through 10.

Several times when I've been nymph fishing for other species, bright sockeyes have intercepted my nymphs. I don't want to begin to guess why a sockeye would strike a nymph, and after it happens, I consider it a fluke. But since the first time I hooked a sockeye on a nymph, I've learned that there are several flyfishers, having had the same experience, who intentionally use nymphs for sockeye salmon. I have tried it enough times in enough different places now to recognize that when sockeyes are being tight-lipped a small nymph may be just the ticket to get them to change their mood.

Tactics for Sockeyes

When sockeyes are in their prime, mint bright and fresh from the ocean, it's often much more difficult to get them to strike at a fly than when they are displaying the aggressiveness related to spawning. Proper presentation is of paramount importance when trying to entice sockeyes to hit a fly. Casting across and slightly downstream allowing the wet fly to drift naturally is the preferred presentation. This does not at once appear to be very difficult, as almost every flyfisher uses this typical wet-fly swing in many different situations. But to be able to hook sockeyes consistently you'll need to go beyond the rudimentary skills associated with this technique.

For starters, you'll need to present the fly at the exact depth at which the salmon are holding. Passing the fly above or below the level of the fish will rarely result in a strike from sockeye salmon. To further complicate matters, it is always better, though not always absolutely necessary, to present the fly broadside to the fish. These two objectives, while not extremely difficult to master, require that the angler fish with great concentration instead of falling into the chuck-it-and-chance-it attitude displayed by many anglers.

Flyfishing for sockeye.

Once the fly is being presented properly, detecting the strike is no small feat because sockeyes will rarely belt a fly. The typical strike from a sockeye will take the form of nothing more than a slight hesitation of the line as the salmon quickly mouths and then spits out the fly. Sensing this soft take is difficult, as it is when fishing with a nymph. It often takes a fair amount of practice to get used to detecting the strike.

All of these factors can be made much more difficult if the angler doesn't position himself in the best possible spot to present the fly to the fish. Slightly up and across stream from the holding salmon, if it is at all possible to get there, is by far the best place. Of course, if you can see the fish, it's easier to get into a good position, and this is one reason why you should always thoroughly search the water with the aid of polarized glasses before you begin to fish.

If the lighting is poor or the water is glacial or otherwise discolored, you will have to guess where the fish may be holding and position yourself in a good spot to fish the potential holding water. This is where being able to read the water is a valuable asset. A description of how to read the water can be put into words, but there's no substitute for spending time on the water. In most instances this is the only way to develop the skill of reading water.

One of the best ways to acquire a feel for where the salmon are holding is to carefully observe them when it is possible to do so in clear water. Take good mental notes on the type of water where the fish are holding, and then fish that same kind of water in streams where the fish are not visible. A good rule of thumb when you're fishing for any salmon in Alaska is to fish the spots that have the slowest currents. Having entered freshwater, salmon are at one brief stop in a long journey, and they will take refuge from the stronger, tiring currents whenever they can.

Other than learning where salmon will lie by watching them, very clear streams offer some other advantages. In some situations you will be able to watch your fly throughout the entire drift. This will allow you to present it easily at the correct depth, and you may also be able to actually watch the salmon take the fly. Obviously, this makes it easier to set the hook, and it may help you to develop that sixth sense which is needed to detect a strike when both the fly and the fish are unseen.

There will be times when you seem to be doing everything right but you can't get the fish to strike. This is not uncommon, and people who frequently fish for sockeye salmon come to regard it as one of the species's most distinctive traits. Typically, the action will slow down considerably after you catch a few, and then for a period which can last from 20 minutes to a couple of hours, the fish will refuse everything that you put in front of them. Later it's as if someone flipped a switch, and suddenly they begin striking again.

Strangely enough, this behavior is usually consistent throughout an entire area of a stream. Anglers positioned both upstream and downstream, as much as 100 yards away, will most likely experience the same blank periods and the same blocks of time when the action is fast. This on-again, off-again behavior often occurs well inland beyond where there is any tidal influence, and it doesn't seem to follow any regular pattern. Nor does there seem to be any visible environmental clue, such as changing weather conditions, that trips sockeyes into hitting and non-hitting modes.

Often during these slack periods, human nature prevails, and most flyfishers rush to try out every fly in their vest. But your best tactic is to simply stick with the fly that had previously produced. Often it's just a short time before it will begin working again.

Equipment for Sockeyes

When you have sockeye salmon in mind, a seven-weight outfit is a good choice. As with any salmon outfit, a full range of lines is extremely important for success, because conditions can change dramatically from stream to stream and from day to day. With sinking and sink-tip lines, leaders of four feet in length work fine, and with floating lines anything longer than seven feet is seldom necessary. Leader strength and design is always a matter of personal preference, and I frequently try new materials and different tapers. My tippet breaking strength, though, usually stays the same and is typically eight or 10 pounds for sockeye salmon. Any reel that is compatible with a seven-weight rod will probably hold somewhere in the vicinity of 100 yards of backing, which is adequate for sockeye salmon.

POLAR SHRIMP

Chapter 4
Pink Salmon

Occasionally I would be able to strip the fly all the way in without getting a strike. Had I kept count, the numbers would have probably been something like nine or 10 fish for every dozen casts. The fly I was using, a size 8 Polar Shrimp, had been torn to shreds. It had no wing or tail left, and only half of the hook shank was still covered with chenille. In almost any other situation, I would have replaced the fly many casts ago, but today I wanted to see how long these pink salmon would stay interested in the remnants of a fly.

Three more fish succumbed to the tattered fly. The last of the three struck the Polar Shrimp when nothing remained except a quarter-inch piece of chenille hanging from the bend of the hook. I gave the fish six chances, six casts, to hit the bare hook. None did. I didn't really expect them to strike the bare hook, but then again, I don't think it would have surprised me if they had.

Pinks—usually found in large numbers.

It was one of July's bluebird days. The kind of day when the chamber of commerce and the visitor's information bureau take all of their pictures. Anyone who was fishing one of these little streams that drained into Resurrection Bay might think that they had stumbled across a flyfishing utopia. Everything was right—60 degree temperatures, blue skies, no wind, and enough fish so that nearly every cast resulted in a strike.

Of course, not every day spent fishing for pink salmon is this nice. It could rain, it might not be as warm, and the wind could make casting a challenge. But there are two things that are consistent with regard to pink salmon: they are usually found in very large numbers, and they never seem to be difficult to catch.

While in the ocean, pink salmon are silver-blue on top, silver on their sides, and white on their belly. Their backs have numerous black, oval-shaped spots as does the entire tail from top to bottom. Finding the large, oval-shaped spots on both lobes of the tail is a quick and easy way to distinguish a pink salmon from its other salmon relatives.

Once pink salmon reach freshwater they quickly lose their silver color. The bright, handsome fish of the ocean become very dark gray on their backs, and on their sides they display blotches of brown, gray, and green. The males develop a large hump behind their head, hence their nickname, humpbacked salmon or, more commonly, humpies.

This large, grotesque hump combined with their blotchy gray-green coloring doesn't do much for their appearance or for the perception of them held by the public. In fact, most flyfishers don't hold them in too high regard once the fish have entered freshwater. The reason for this is quite simple. Normally, pink salmon don't travel very far from the ocean to spawn, and in some areas spawning takes place in the intertidal zone. In accordance with being such a short-distance fish, their bodies "color up" and deteriorate rapidly once in freshwater. Some even begin to show their spawning colors while they're still in saltwater.

Pink Salmon: When and Where

Pink salmon (*Oncorhynchus gorbuscha*) are the smallest of Alaska's salmon. Anything over eight pounds is a real monster, and fish are most commonly in the two- to five-pound range. The waters around Kodiak Island and throughout southeast Alaska are home to much larger fish. In some of these areas the average pink salmon may be close to six pounds. However, what pink salmon generally lack in size, they make up for in sheer numbers.

Due to the two distinct stocks of odd-year and even-year fish, there can be a big difference in yearly run totals. In many places the even-year run (1996, 1998, 2000, etc.) far outnumbers the fish returning on the odd years. In the even years, some streams get such a large return of fish in relation to the stream's size that the pinks can choke the mouth of the stream. Now I know that this "choking the mouth of a stream" sounds like a fishing cliché, but in this case it's no exaggeration. Pinks can be packed in so tightly that fishing for them, or any other species of fish, can be nearly impossible. Any fly cast into the water, unless it is

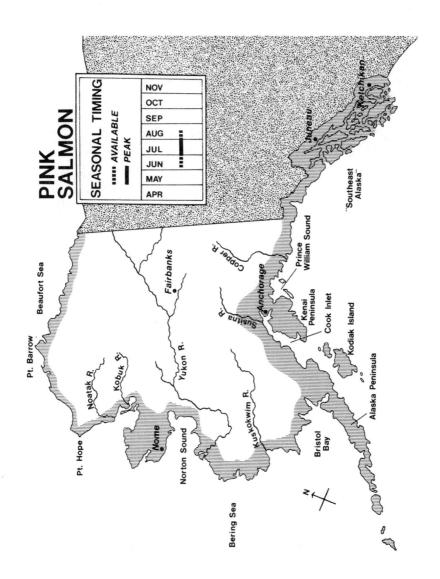

PINK SALMON

SEASONAL TIMING

..... AVAILABLE

—— PEAK

NOV	
OCT	
SEP	
AUG	▪▪
JUL	█
JUN	▪█▪
MAY	
APR	

River mouth: best place for pink salmon.

immediately struck by a salmon, will most assuredly foul-hook a fish when it is retrieved.

What is perhaps the strangest bit of fishing advice you'll ever hear is a result of the foul-hooking problem in these pink salmon traffic jams. During a strong run of pinks it's sometimes best to fish in those sections of stream that have less fish. That's right. Fish where there are fewer fish, and you'll have better odds of catching them!

Timing your fishing is critical in years of pink abundance. Because they can form a veritable log jam at the mouth of a creek and because they deteriorate rapidly once in freshwater, it's best to fish for them very early in the run. The ideal time is the first week that the pinks begin to show up in freshwater. The best area of the river to fish is its lower reaches—the area that is still influenced by the tides. Male pink salmon are normally larger than the females, and the first males to reach freshwater are usually the largest fish of the run, another good reason to get in on the early action.

The intertidal zone of a river will give you the best shot at a really fresh pink salmon. It also has a few inherent

Small pink salmon.

dangers that have to be mentioned here. Alaska's coastline is home to some extreme tidal fluctuations. In fact, Cook Inlet has a maximum diurnal range which is just shy of 39 feet. This is an extreme, but it does point out that you have to pay attention when you're fishing tidal waters.

It's easy to wade through waist-deep water and then climb onto a rock or shelf which puts you shin deep in water and gives you a much welcomed elevated casting platform. What isn't easy, though, is when you suddenly realize that you're still on your perch, but the water is now lapping against your wading belt. Turning and looking toward shore you'll find that it is much farther away, and all that waist-deep water you initially waded through is much deeper than you are tall. Take it from me, swimming in the waters of coastal Alaska—even during the summer—isn't something you want to do. Aside from being a chilling experience, it's also very dangerous. Carry a tide book, learn how to read it, and pay attention when fishing intertidal areas.

The mudflats of Turnagain Arm also warrant special mention. Two popular rivers to fish for pink salmon there— Bird Creek and Ingram Creek—meander through hundreds of yards of exposed mudflats during a low tide. You may see people that wander way out on the mudflats, but I would recommend against it. Although the footing may seem solid, there are times just prior to an incoming tide when the substrate can quickly turn into the consistency of fresh cement. It's amusing at these times to become so stuck that you pull your foot right out of your hip wader. Getting stuck, however, can lead to tragic circumstances if you're unable to free yourself and there's an incoming tide. Several years ago a woman lost her life under such circumstances. Play it safe and stay on solid ground.

Pink salmon will return to watersheds from the south-ernmost areas of Alaska's panhandle all the way up to the Bering Sea. Like other salmon, the run timing for pinks is largely dependent upon the location, and they may be found in freshwater anytime from June until September. Overall, whether you are at the mouth of the Yukon River or on Kodiak Island, July is the best month for fresh pink salmon.

If you ask a guide or outfitter questions concerning the run timing for pinks or any other salmon, they'll probably speak in terms of the peak of the run. The peak usually refers to the time period, ranging from a few days to a few weeks, when the greatest number of that particular salmon species will be in freshwater. After the peak, stragglers may still be coming in, but all the salmon in the rivers will be on the downside as far as physical condition is concerned. Fishing at the peak time will give you an opportunity to fish for a great number of fish, but keep in mind, the best time for the largest and freshest pink salmon is early in the run. For the best pink salmon fishing, time your arrival before the peak of the run.

The Life Cycle of Pink Salmon

The pink salmon's life cycle exhibits a consistency that all the other salmon of Alaska lack. Almost all of the fish return to spawn at age two. Only rarely are three-year-old fish found. In fact, the pinks are so set in their ways that fish of the odd-numbered years and fish of the even-numbered years maintain some morphological and genetic differences.

Spawning behavior is much like that of other Alaskan salmon. The female does the redd building while an attendant male spends his time chasing off other males. After depositing the eggs, the female begins to dig upstream of the redd, covering the eggs in the process. The eggs hatch sometime in mid-winter and remain in the stream gravel while in the alevin stage.

When spring arrives, the fry break out of the gravel and immediately begin their seaward migration. Most of this movement takes place at night, and sometimes they may have such short distances to go that they reach the ocean on their first night of travel. In the ocean, they'll feed for 18 months and then return to their home streams. Many, though, will wander and wind up in a different stream. All species of Alaska's salmon wander to some degree, but the pink salmon do it to a greater extent than any of the others.

Fly Patterns for Pink Salmon

Many of the fly patterns that are mentioned in the other salmon chapters can be used with great success for pink salmon. Most notable among them are the Comets and Bosses in various colors. If you were creating a fly selection with just pink salmon in mind, you'd want to include patterns that have some flash to them. Whether it is a body of bright tinsel or a wing or tail of Flashabou or Krystal Flash, a little bit of flash seems to be a key ingredient in creating an effective fly for pink salmon.

Of course, when putting together a flashy fly selection, your first and most logical choice would have to be the Flash Fly. Most often thought of as a silver or king salmon fly, the Flash Fly is an extremely effective pink salmon pattern. Slight changes in the hackle color, say from red to orange, don't seem to either increase or decrease the effectiveness of the fly. However, there are times when a Flash Fly with very dark hackle, such as black or purple, will produce more strikes than ones with lighter colors. For some reason most flyfishers do not tie Flash Flies in any color other than silver, the color of the original Flash Fly. I recently have begun to tie them using purple, gold, or green Flashabou instead of silver. The resulting flies not only look very promising, but the few times that I have used them, they worked extremely well.

Many of the smolt patterns, since most of them have either silver tinsel or Mylar bodies, also take their share of pink salmon. The Blue Smolt and the Black-Nosed Dace are especially good patterns to use at creek mouths where fresh-water meets saltwater. The Thunder Creek series of flies also works quite well, particularly if some flash is added to the standard patterns. My favorite color combinations are blue over white and green over white. Pink salmon fresh from the ocean may still harbor the instinct which causes them to strike small baitfish as a feeding response. I suppose that may be why these small flashy patterns, which could easily be confused with baitfish, work so well.

It would be difficult to create a fly selection for any of Alaska's salmon and not include patterns that are predominantly orange. Any of the double-egg flies, as well as the single-egg patterns, will work for pink salmon. Equally effective are other flies that are mostly orange in color, such as the Polar Shrimp, the Kispiox Special, and the Thor. It goes without saying that if you wanted to use them up on pinks, many of the colorful flies created for steelhead will catch pink salmon.

The many colors of the Alaskabou, such as red, pink, and chartreuse and white, do a good job of attracting the

Bright pink salmon.

attention of pink salmon, but they are not often used for pinks. I think this is mainly due to the fact that they are most often carried in very large sizes (3/0 and 1/0), and fly-fishers are hesitant to throw such a big fly to the diminutive pinks. Rest assured, a pink salmon can easily engulf a very large fly if it wants to.

This brings us to the topic of hook size. I prefer small hooks for pinks, sizes 6, 8, and even 10. My size selection has little to do with what is best for pink salmon. Pinks don't necessarily prefer small flies over larger flies—most of the time they show no preference. Rather it is what best suits me. On a light outfit, casting a lightly-weighted size 8 fly is much more enjoyable than tossing around a size 1/0 fly. Consequently, I stick with the smaller sizes. The only other consideration that may influence your choice of hooks is nearness to saltwater. Fishing river mouths for fresh pinks, you may have the opportunity to cast into brackish water or saltwater, and you may want to use hooks with a non-corrosive finish.

Equipment for Pink Salmon

Don't be fooled by some flyfishers' disdain for the pink salmon. For their size, they'll fight gamely when taken with the right tackle. More often than not, they are caught with the same outfits used for silver, sockeye, and chum salmon. However, under almost all circumstances, I would prefer to go after pinks with a five-weight system. It's much more fun to let pinks rip off some line and put a full bend in the rod rather than subduing them with an eight-weight rod. A single-action fly reel with a simple click-pawl drag system that can be being palmed, complemented with a nine-foot rod is a good setup to use for pink salmon. With an outfit such as this, you could catch them all day long, be very appreciative of their fight, and yet still release them before they reach the point of exhaustion.

As usual, water velocity and depth will dictate the most advantageous type of line to use. Generally, in the lower reaches of streams and at tidewater, pink salmon will move up and down in the water column quite freely to take a fly. Floating and moderate-density sink-tip lines are usually all that is needed. I adjust my leader strength in accordance with the average size of the fish being caught. Rarely, though, will I drop below six-pound test, just in case there is a monster lurking out there somewhere. Close enough to the ocean, a pink salmon may try to make a run for open water, but as long as you have around 100 yards of 20-pound Dacron behind your fly line, you'll have more than enough line.

Dead-drifting a fly through a likely holding spot is often the only technique that is needed to catch pink salmon in Alaska. The fly doesn't have to come as critically close to the fish as it often needs to for sockeyes and chums. Retrieving the fly in short bursts is often very effective, and this is the preferred technique to use when pinks are milling around in tidewater areas that have very little current.

In general, you will not need a large assortment of flies or any specialized gear to fish successfully for pink salmon. Just remember to try for them early in the run and in the lowest reaches of the stream. They are the most numerous of all Alaska's salmon, so you should have no trouble finding them. And once you do, you will be delighted with the amount of fun that you can have catching these three- to five-pound fish until your arms grow tired.

SPARKLE SHRIMP

Chapter 5
Chum Salmon

Even if you've spent a lot of time reading flyfishing literature, you may never have encountered references to chum
salmon. If you do find a mention of them, it will probably
be nothing more than a passing phrase, something like, the
fishing was great, and there were also chum salmon present. Some writers are more blunt and state simply that the
chum salmon is not considered a sport fish.

One day I was showing two flyfishers around Prince
William Sound, and I decided to take them to a small creek
mouth so that they could try their luck with chum salmon.
When I mentioned this over the drone of the outboard
engine, neither of them looked too enthusiastic. They both
had a sort of bewildered look on their faces, a look that I'm
used to seeing when I mention chum salmon to flyfishers.

We arrived at the creek mouth three hours before high
tide. I dropped them off on a rocky point, and then I took the
boat around to the back side where there was some protected
water. By the time I'd secured the boat and walked around

the point they had already caught and released a couple of Dolly Varden, and they were busy playing two more. There weren't any chum salmon around, but they weren't upset. They were quite pleased with the Dolly Varden fishing. Switching from their eight-weights to their five-weights, they headed farther upstream to look for more Dollies.

I walked back to the end of the point and began making long casts with a green-and-white bucktail that had a little bit of Flashabou added to it. I hadn't made three casts when I heard a yell and the sweet sound a reel makes when the line is quickly being peeled off. I turned and watched. From my great vantage point, I could clearly see a chum streak by with an orange-colored fly stuck in the corner of its mouth and a green fly line slicing through the water behind it. A five-weight rod wasn't the most appropriate tool to be using for chum salmon, and it took what seemed like hours to land that fish. Finally I got into position to restrain the fish for the angler, remove the fly, and switch places with him so he could quickly hold it up for a photo. It was a hook-jawed male of about 12 pounds.

The tide had continued to move in, making the lower reaches of the stream very wide, and we could see more chums making their way upstream. In a few moments each one of us had hooked into chums. With a typical Alaskan weather change taking place (one that didn't look good), we had to cut our time with the chums short and make our way back to the boat. After we were underway, heading for more sheltered waters, the two anglers cursed the weather for interrupting their fishing. The following day we were due back in town, and we didn't have the opportunity to cast for any chum salmon on the way back.

The next week I received a frantic phone call. The two anglers had gotten some more time off from work, and they wondered if I could take them back out to tackle some more chums. I wasn't able to go, but I set them up so that they could go on their own. They did, they had a great time, and they have been going out for chums ever since. Two more flyfishers had become aware of the great sport provided by chum salmon.

In the ocean the adult chum (*Oncorhynchus keta*) are easily distinguished from other salmon by the lack of spots

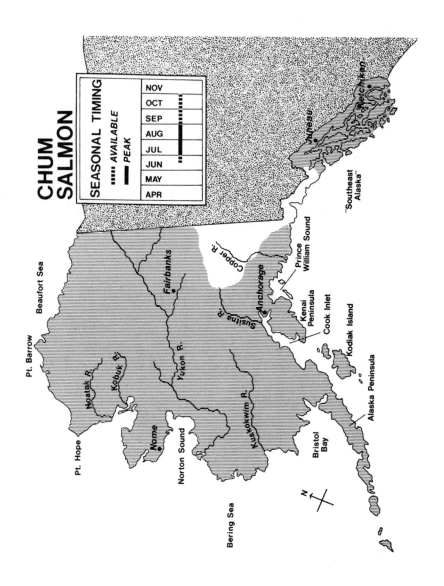

CHUM SALMON

SEASONAL TIMING

..... AVAILABLE

▬ PEAK

NOV	
OCT	
SEP	
AUG	
JUL	
JUN	
MAY	
APR	

River mouth: good place to find chum salmon.

on their tails and backs. Their bellies and sides are silvery white, and their backs are a shiny dark blue or green. Once ready to spawn, chums will turn darker shades of olive, brown, and red on their bellies and backs, while their sides will sport irregular bars or stripes that are for the most part greenish-olive. The males develop a large conspicuous kype that is loaded with canine-looking teeth. After seeing the fish in this stage of development, most people assume that it is their caniniform teeth that are responsible for their alternative common name, dog salmon. Actually this name stems from the fact that chum salmon were, and still are in some places, a major food source for the dog teams of the native people—hence the name dog salmon.

Chums: Where and When

Some chums spawn in the lower reaches of rivers not far from the ocean. But others, in particular those that enter the Yukon River, will travel 2,000 miles to Teslin Lake on the Yukon and British Columbia border. The chums that make this long journey remain silver bright even after they have been in freshwater for quite a while. In other areas where chums may only go a short distance to spawn, they'll begin to show shades of their spawning colors even before they reach freshwater.

Chum salmon can be found throughout Alaska from the Southeast to the northwest Bering Sea. The Noatak and the Kobuk rivers have runs of chum salmon that number close to one million fish each, while the Yukon River and its tributaries support an even greater run. Chum salmon are typically considered fall spawners, but their run timing varies tremendously over their wide range. They may be present in freshwater anytime from July through October. If your main interest is chum salmon, it would be highly advisable to contact a local guide, lodge, or outfitter to get specific information on the run timing for the location you'll be fishing.

The Life Cycle of Chums

The female, as with other species of Pacific salmon, has the responsibility of digging the redd. Once it's done, she may mate with one or more males. These males may also attend more than one female. The length of time it takes the eggs to hatch is largely dependent upon the water temperature. When they do hatch, the alevins will stay in the gravel

Chum salmon. Duane Marler

until their egg sac is absorbed, which may take anywhere from two to three months.

As soon as the young emerge from the gravel, they begin their seaward migration. In this respect they are similar to pink salmon, which also spend only a short amount of time in freshwater while they are juveniles. Once in saltwater the chums begin to grow rapidly, and weights of eight to 12 pounds are common after three or four years. As with other aspects of the chum salmon's life cycle, their stay at sea is highly variable—some will return after three years while others will not return for four or five.

Fly Patterns for Chums

Without the rich history that so many other sport fish have, there are no well-known flies that have been developed specifically with chum salmon in mind. However, you don't have to worry, because there are plenty of flies that will entice chums to strike. Comets and Bosses of several different colors are usually quite effective. The Polar Shrimp, the Sparkle Shrimp, the Flash Fly, almost any colorful streamer such as the Mickey Finn, and the Orange-and-White Wiggle-tail are also good choices for chums. The many variations of the smolt pattern, for whatever reason, have also found their way into a chum's mouth on more than one occasion.

Although they will hit a wide variety of flies, there are times on certain rivers when chums become very color selective. One five-day trip on the Togiak River really drove this point home. For three of the five days I had no trouble hooking chums on nearly any fly that I used. The other two days, however, were completely different. The only fly patterns that I had any luck with were those that were predominantly chartreuse in color. The specific pattern seemed to matter little. This same scenario—although the color was hot pink, not chartreuse—has occurred a couple of other times on different rivers. I've only encountered chums that were color selective on a few occasions, and the odds are, that unless you come to Alaska year after year with an emphasis on fishing for chum salmon, you probably won't run across the situation.

There are probably hundreds of fly patterns, yet to be

named, that can be used with good success for chums. If you have the urge to create your own patterns, remember to combine flash with some outlandish colors and you'll probably have a good chum fly. Hook size is usually not critical. Most of the flies that I tie for chum salmon are on hook sizes 2 and 4.

I think chums can be enticed into striking just about any fly that you have in your collection that may be intended for other Alaskan salmon. Double-egg patterns in various hues of orange always seem to work in freshwater. Single-egg patterns, although I rarely use them for salmon, will also work. I even remember a day when I caught two—not one, but two—chum salmon on a yellow bass popper.

When the fish seem to be hitting anything you throw at them, I tend to try some really crazy flies. The yellow bass popper was a leftover in my vest from a Florida fishing excursion, and when I saw it, I couldn't resist trying it out for at least of a couple of casts. When an eight-pound male chum took it right off the surface, I thought I had just witnessed the fluke of flukes. About half an hour later another male of the same size did the same thing. Two other people witnessed this, but they laugh so much when I tell the story that other people can't tell if I'm pulling their legs or not. It did happen, though, and since then, I've greatly increased my use of poppers.

I began fishing bass poppers over bright chum salmon whenever I had the opportunity to do so, and with a little fine tuning, the results kept getting better and better. Lots of colors—including yellow, orange, red, and bright green—worked, but by far the best producer is hot pink. The size of the popper doesn't seem to matter, but the way it floats does. High-floating poppers don't work as well as those that break the surface and sit lower in the water. The best have a very buoyant head and a trailing combination of marabou, saddle hackle, and rubber legs that protrude below the water's surface. My favorite has a pink bullet-shaped head with a tail three times as long as the head. The tail is made of pink marabou, two black saddle hackles, and six strands of white rubber legs.

Chums will occasionally strike a floating fly while it's dead-drifting, but more often than not, they prefer a waking fly. As with greased-line fishing for steelhead, the speed at which the fly wakes is important, but I'm not prepared to recommend—nor do I know—the exact speed in feet per second that is best. Rather, I've found that along flatwater stretches of rivers where the water is moving at perhaps three to four miles an hour, a cast made at approximately 45 degrees downstream, with a slight downstream mend to put a belly in the line, results in a swing of about the right speed. It is possible to drag the fly through the water too fast, so when you're trying to get a feel for the right speed, it's best to work with a nearly dead-drifting fly and every couple of casts gradually increase the fly's speed. Obviously, when you get a strike you've found the right speed, but if the fish repeatedly boil behind the fly without getting hooked, it's best to back off a bit and slow the fly down.

Duplication of any type of experiment is a good way to check the validity of its results, and I was pleased to learn that other anglers were trying dry flies for chum salmon with similar results. The only noticeable difference in style and technique was that other anglers I discussed this with were using flies made of brightly-colored spun deer hair instead of bass poppers. I don't doubt that the deer hair creations are equally effective, but taking into account the difficulty of making deer hair bugs and the fact that poppers float forever without getting waterlogged, I'm going to stick with my poppers.

Tactics for Chums

In some situations, fishing for chum salmon can be very frustrating because they act like sockeye salmon. This is especially true when they're in very shallow, clear water and are not present in very large numbers. At these times, using the same tactics employed for sockeye salmon will hold you in good stead. Remember to get into the best position to cast to the fish, keep a short, controlled line, repeatedly present the fly at the exact depth of the holding fish, and lastly, be prepared for a very subtle strike. The size of fly used under these conditions seems to matter little. Sizes 8 through 1/0 are taken with equal frequency.

Fortunately large schools of chum salmon, numbering in

Bright chum with king salmon. Duane Marler

the hundreds, are commonly found, and there are always plenty of them eager to hit a fly. At first, the idea of schools of a hundred or more salmon may seem an exaggeration, but during the height of any of the salmon runs in Alaska, groups of fish this large are common. In major spawning tributaries, groups of fish that number in the thousands are common. When you do encounter a mass of fish such as this, hook-ups will most likely be very frequent. This is when you can successfully fish those gaudy creations full of tinsel, Flashabou, Krystal Flash, and brightly-colored saddle hackle. Maybe it has something to do with group dynamics. Who knows for sure, but under these conditions chum salmon are very susceptible to big, bright flies. An Alaskabou or a Popsicle would be an excellent fly choice.

Fishing to a big school of chums means that you'll be fishing the water as opposed to singling out one target. You should plan to cover as much water with your fly as the school occupies. Get into a position where you can make a presentation by casting straight across, quartering down-

and-across, and then almost straight downstream. This progression of casting angles should allow you to cover an entire school of fish. Start with the ones that are holding closest and directly across the stream from you, and finish with the fish holding directly downstream from you.

A typical wet-fly swing works well. Strikes may occur at any point in the drift, from the moment you take up the slack until the fly hangs motionless in the current below you. Letting the fly hang for a second or two after the drift has been completed is also a good tactic. Chum salmon will often move forward and hit a fly that is not moving. At other times they may hit the fly as it is being retrieved. If you find this to be the case, then on your next cast you should begin to strip retrieve the fly while it is still drifting. Experiment with different retrieve sequences, varying both the length of the pull and the speed at which it is executed. You just may find one particular retrieve sequence that results in a banner day.

Equipment for Chums

While record specimens may reach sizes upwards of 20 pounds, on the average chum salmon in Alaska weigh only a couple more pounds than sockeyes, and the same gear can be used for both. An eight-weight rod with a complementary reel is quite satisfactory. An array of lines, from floating to quick-sinking varieties, is always recommended to meet changing conditions. Leaders having terminal points with a breaking strength of eight to 12 pounds are a good choice. I have never had a chum spool out more than 100 yards of backing, but it wouldn't hurt to have more. You might be very thankful for having the extra yardage if you hook into a very large chum in swift currents. The Alaskan state record is 32 pounds.

A word about lines is in order here. I get the most enjoyment when casting a floating line and prefer to use one whenever possible. The reason for this is quite simple. Often I'll be fishing close to another flyfisher who's using a different type of line, and we'll both have roughly the same success rate. In the past I used some type of sinking line a majority of the time when I was fishing for salmon, but with the exception of king salmon fishing, I now rely more heavily upon a floating line. It's simply a matter of style and technique rather than a marked increase in fish-catching efficiency, and I'm hesitant to say that this will be the norm for anyone else's salmon fishing.

Take, for example, a situation where you need to present the fly at a depth of four feet in moderate water velocities. This can be accomplished in at least two ways. One flyfisher may use a sink-tip line with a short leader. Another flyfisher may use a floating line with a long leader and a weighted fly to fish the same depth. Both methods have their proponents, and both techniques will catch fish. Taking the conditions you observe into consideration, it is up to you to decide which technique to use. The one you deem best suited for the immediate situation may frequently not be your favorite method, but don't handicap yourself by fishing only one method or by carrying only one line. This holds true not only in fishing for chum but for all the other species of salmon that inhabit Alaskan waters.

In regard to both flies and techniques, there are not any real standards where chums are concerned. It goes without saying that the chum salmon is truly the underdog of Alaska's salmon. This is largely due to the fact that flyfishers, and anglers in general, have not paid too much attention to them. This presents a unique situation for the flyfisher who enjoys trying new techniques. The flyfisher who does experiment has the chance to develop new and effective techniques for chum salmon.

If you're still unclear as to why flyfishers do not pay more attention to the chum salmon, you're not alone. Somewhere along the line most flyfishers have decided that chum salmon are not worthy opponents, but things are beginning to change. Some flyfishers are taking a new look at chums. This, I believe, is largely because of the advent of taking them with topwater flies, which seems to elevate their status in the minds of many flyfishers. Whether they happen to be the target species for a particular trip or just an incidental catch, I have always thoroughly enjoyed taking the hard-fighting chum salmon on a fly.

FLASH FLY

Chapter 6
Silver Salmon

High tide was still three hours away, but every couple of minutes a new school of fish would swim into view. The stream's clear water was only about four feet deep, and I could easily spot the dark shapes of salmon against the bottom of pea-sized gravel. I had strategically positioned myself at a fork in the stream. I hoped that the salmon would hesitate in their upstream progress while they decided whether to stay with the main current or head up the smaller tributary stream. The next wave of fish did just that, and I found myself staring into the water at a group of about two dozen silver salmon not more than 30 feet away.

My nine-and-a-half foot, eight-weight graphite rod barely flexed with the short cast. I targeted the fish closest to me, and my fly, a size 2 Flash Fly, plopped into the water 10 feet upstream from the salmon. The fly was a little off its mark, and I quickly stripped in a foot or two of line so that the fly would drift right into the fish. But the fish I had cast to never had a shot at the fly. Just as I finished the quick strip, a salmon from the other side of the school raced over and belted it.

Almost instantly, the fish leaped clear of the water, splashed back down, and raced right at me. Instinctively, I reeled madly while back-peddling for shore. The commotion scared it, and the fish turned and shot up the small tributary stream. Not satisfied with that direction, the salmon then swam out of the stream just as quickly as it had entered it. Next, the fish peeled off the line that I had regained and headed up the main branch of the creek. I leaned back on the rod to add some pressure, and this quickly brought the salmon back into the air. After hitting the water, the salmon lost its desire to swim upstream and instead the line flew through my guides as the fish swam downstream. Well into my backing now, this salmon wasn't stopping—it was heading for saltwater.

I followed from the stream bank, regaining line as I went. Several minutes later, I had tired the fish enough to bring it to shore. I knelt down in a foot of water and grasped its tail. My free hand reached for my pliers, and just as I removed the fly from its upper jaw, the 12-pound silver shot back into the main current of the stream.

When I stood up, I realized that I had come within 50 yards of the saltwater of Cook Inlet. I had followed that silver salmon over 100 yards. Instead of walking back upstream, I decided to fish right where I was. A couple of casts later another silver salmon slammed into the fly and left a torpedo-like wake as it sped upstream. I didn't land that fish, but I did land three or four others in the next hour or so.

I was so completely engrossed with my fishing that I hadn't checked to see how my fishing partners were doing upstream. About that time I heard some shouting and recognized the voices of my companions. It must be dinner time, I thought. However, there were still fish swirling near the surface, and I was determined to make a couple more casts before I acknowledged the shouts of my friends. Then the pitch of their voices changed, the shouts were much louder, and they came in rapid succession. I turned to yell back at them, and when I did, my eyes quickly picked up the subject of all their

...1. There was a brown bear moving rather fast, and he ...ding across the beach right in my direction.

...bear was steadily closing the distance between us, and ...se he was paying attention to my friends, he hadn't ...noticed me. I waved my arms and let go with a very ...ud, long string of words. Some of the words were incomprehensible, and the others aren't really fit to print. Basically, I let the bear know that I was there. I also recommended that he not bother with me because I was harmless, and I would give him the entire river mouth if he wanted it. It did the trick. The bear skidded to a stop, stared at me, looked back toward my friends, and then turned and raced back across the beach for the safety of the trees.

I turned and reeled in my line. A silver salmon rolled next to the far shore. My friends were laughing loudly. I was laughing too—well, sort of laughing. Another silver salmon broke the water's surface, but I decided that those fish could wait. It must be time for dinner.

The silver salmon (*Oncorhynchus kisutch*) also goes by the name of coho salmon. Throughout Alaska, though, they are usually referred to as silvers, and in mid- to late July, flyfishers anxiously await the magic words—the silvers are in. These sleek fish are easily recognized by their brilliant silver color and the presence of a few small black spots along their backs and on the top lobes of their tails. After spending some time in freshwater, the males, like other Alaskan salmon, develop a hooked jaw and both sexes turn a dark red color. Average weights of silvers vary with their locality, but eight- to 10-pound fish are the most common. However, it's not at all unusual to catch silvers of over 15 pounds, and every season 20-pound fish are caught. The Alaskan record is 26 pounds.

Silvers: Where and When

Silvers are found from southernmost southeast Alaska all the way north to Point Hope. Although some will venture far inland, generally they prefer, and are most abundant in, shorter coastal streams. September and October are the best months to fish for silvers in the Southeast. There

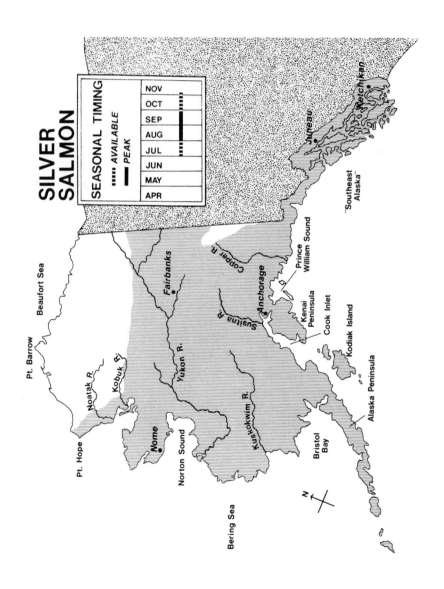

SILVER
SALMON

SEASONAL TIMING

..... AVAILABLE
━━━ PEAK

| NOV |
| OCT |
| SEP |
| AUG |
| JUL |
| JUN |
| MAY |
| APR |

Beaufort Sea

Pt. Barrow

Fairbanks

Copper R.

Prince
William Sound

Anchorage

Susitna R.

Kenai
Peninsula

Cook Inlet

Kodiak Island

"Southeast
Alaska"

Ketchikan

Juneau

Noatak R.

Kobuk R.

Pt. Hope

Yukon R.

Nome

Norton Sound

Kuskokwim R.

Bristol
Bay

Alaska Peninsula

Bering Sea

N

are several streams in the Juneau and
have good runs. Many other places
east also have silver salmon, but th
and the Italio rivers in the Yakut

August is a good time to sea
liam Sound. Here, fishing can
or right in the saltwater bay
and the Nellie Martin Riv
lent spots for silvers.

The arrival of silver s
fishers who regularly fish the
Inlet. Scattered reports of silvers b
action really doesn't start to heat up until
that. The popular Kenai River receives a strong run
salmon, as do several other road-accessible streams on the
Kenai Peninsula. Most of the tributaries to the Susitna
River in upper Cook Inlet also get runs of silvers, but they
are subjected to fairly heavy fishing pressure. Cook Inlet's
west side has fewer silver salmon streams, but they get less
fishing pressure. My two picks for Cook Inlet would be the
Chuit River and Silver Salmon Creek.

There are many rivers on Kodiak Island that have superb
silver salmon fishing. Some, such as the Buskin and the
Pasagshak rivers, can be reached via Kodiak's road system.
Access to most of the rivers on Kodiak, though, is only by
boat or plane. The most notable of these rivers is the Karluk.

Western Alaska, from Bristol Bay north to Norton Sound,
has many rivers that offer excellent flyfishing opportunities
for silver salmon. Starting in the south, the flyfisher can
choose from the Ugashik River, the Wood River system, the
Goodnews River, and farther north the Unalakleet and the
Nome rivers. These rivers and their associated tributaries
are great places to go for silvers, but they are by no means
the only places to go. Numerous other watersheds in this
area get strong returns of silver salmon from late July on
into September.

The Life Cycle of Silvers

The female silver salmon begins redd building once the
fish reach their spawning grounds. Driving away other

Releasing a silver salmon.

females near the redd, each female will continue to dig and deposit about 2,500 eggs over a period of several days. The males may then go on to pair up with other females, and both sexes will die shortly after they have completed the spawning process.

When the fry emerge from the gravel, they immediately begin feeding on a variety of small invertebrates. While doing so, a large percentage of the fry begin to swim upstream searching out suitable pools to use as nursery areas. As they grow, these young silvers become very territorial, and they will defend their space against all similar or smaller-sized intruders. This behavior, combined with their desire to eat larger and larger prey, causes the silvers to become very efficient predators. Many young sockeye salmon and other small fish become victims of the juvenile silver's voracious appetite.

Typically these immature silvers will spend one year in freshwater before leaving for the ocean. It is not unusual, though, for some to stay in freshwater for two, three, and even four years. Once they are ready to depart for the ocean, they will lose their parr marks and turn silver in color. Feeding in the ocean will take up the next two or three years of their lives until they return to the streams where they emerged from the gravel.

Fly Patterns for Silvers

The Flash Fly and the silver salmon is probably the most well-known fly-and-fish combination in Alaska. The Flash Fly, although taken by many other species of fish, is the mainstay of a flyfisher's assortment of flies used for silver salmon. It has a silver Flashabou wing and tail, a wrapped Poly Flash body, and a saddle hackle collar in either orange or red. For silver salmon I prefer a size 2, but one size in either direction doesn't seem to matter to the fish.

As with any successful fly pattern, over time many variations on the original are developed, and the Flash Fly is no exception. Almost any color saddle hackle is now substituted for the red or orange used on the early versions. Many different colors of Flashabou and Poly Flash are also now used. Of all these variations, an all-purple version has become second in popularity to the original silver one.

The Maraflash Fly, a variation of the Flash Fly, is also good for silver salmon. It is tied similarly to the Flash Fly except that some marabou is added to the wing. It is frequently tied with orange or red marabou and less commonly with white or purple.

Since the silver salmon's alternative name is coho salmon, many people are under the impression that the Coho Fly is a good pattern to use for silvers. Actually, the Coho Fly is used mainly for sockeye salmon on the Russian River. The typical Coho Fly is crudely tied with wings of bucktail, and the head is often wrapped with dental floss. While the Coho Fly may at any time interest some game fish, most experienced Alaskan flyfishers do not carry the Coho Fly.

Like king salmon, silvers often show a predisposition for very bright and fluorescent colors. Sparkle Shrimp tied in cerise, chartreuse, and pink are steady producers of silver salmon. Sparkle Shrimp are tied with a matching-colored chenille body and palmered hackle. Pearl Flashabou is tied in for the tail and is left long enough that it can be brought forward and tied off at the head forming a shellback. The most popular hook size for Sparkle Shrimp is size 4.

Everglow Flies are an important part of any Alaskan salmon fly assortment, and their use for silver salmon is no exception. I have found that all of the Everglow colors will work for silvers, but I like two in particular—chartreuse and a combination of orange and white. The materials in a Chartreuse Everglow are all the same color, but for the Orange-and-White Everglow, I use a white body and an orange wing.

All of the Comets and Bosses that are mentioned in the previous chapters can also be used very effectively for silver salmon. Egg patterns, such as the Babine Special and the Two-Egg Sperm Fly, will also do the trick. Not typically considered salmon flies, the Purple Woolly Bugger and the Egg-Sucking Leech are two flies that you also wouldn't want to be without during the silver salmon run.

Silver salmon, under the right conditions, can be taken on dry flies. On very few occasions throughout the season, any one of Alaska's salmon might possibly be coaxed into taking a dry fly, but with the silver salmon it can be a relatively consistent event. You're most likely to get some response to your dry fly if you are fishing over bright silvers—the fresher the better. The best conditions provide clear water four feet or less in depth with a smooth, unriffled surface. Cast quartering downstream so that your fly drags slightly and creates a wake as it drags in the current. Strikes most often come at the apex of the swing.

As for dry flies, large, bulky creations such as Atlantic salmon Bombers, Wulffs, and Humpies can all be used with success. Any of the steelhead dry flies, such as the Steelhead Bee or the Disco Mouse, are also good choices. Sizes range from 2 through 8, but I carry the Wulffs, Humpies, and Steelhead Bee in sizes 8 and 6 and the Bomber and Disco Mouse in size 4. My favorites, however, are the brightly-colored bass poppers that I also use for chum salmon and Walli Wakers tied in fluorescent pink and orange.

Tactics for Silvers

The silver salmon's aggressiveness and willingness to hit a fly will leave any first-time flyfisher for this species with a lasting and favorable impression. Another endearing trait is their propensity to make repeated runs, showing amazing bursts of speed that are often punctuated with aerial cartwheels. Reckless abandon is an appropriate term for the silver salmon's overall style, from the initial hit right through to the end of the fight.

More than half of the time, a fast retrieve draws the most attention on an Alaskan stream during the silver salmon run. To start, you will want to position yourself just up and across stream from the holding fish. From here you can place your fly 10 feet or so upstream of them and then strip the fly in as it drifts toward the fish. I usually start by stripping the fly in four inches at a time at fairly slow intervals. If this fails to produce any reaction, I will increase the length of each strip and decrease the time interval between each strip. Often the fish will show a preference for one particular retrieve sequence, and it may not be until you are making almost continuous, foot-long pulls that the silvers begin to strike.

In clearwater streams, using bright flies with a fast retrieve is a deadly tactic for silvers. You will quickly find that, unlike most of Alaska's other salmon, silvers will roam freely from side to side and upwards in the water to take a fly. Consequently, you will also find that the retrieve, not the depth of the presentation, is the critical component in fishing for silver salmon. You can, of course, take this to an extreme where it will not hold true. For instance, if the fish are holding at the bottom of a pool that is over 10 feet deep, your fly will not attract much attention if it stays within a foot of the surface of the water. Get it down six or seven feet, and then you'll begin to get strikes.

There are times, although it doesn't happen too often, when silvers will not be receptive to bright flies and fast retrieves. This occurs most often when water conditions

Silver salmon at dusk.

are very low and clear. In this situation silvers may avoid
even a closely placed fly. This is a good time to switch to a
darker pattern, such as the Black Boss, and fish it dead drift
just as you would a nymph. Often, a slow retrieve initiated
after the fly has completed its drift will bring strikes. My
favorite flies to use when the fish are acting this way are an
Egg-Sucking Leech, a Purple Woolly Bugger, or a Black
Woolly Worm, all tied on size 4, 3x-long hooks.

It is under these same low and clear water conditions that
you'll have your best opportunity to catch silvers on a dry fly.
I have had silvers burst through four feet of water to slash at

a big dry fly. In water any deeper than five feet, your chances of enticing one to come up decrease greatly. I have also found that broken surface water, as in a riffle or a rapid, or water that is glacially silted, does not afford you with good odds of getting a hit on the surface. Long stretches of stream from three- to five-feet deep with flat unbroken surfaces are the best places to give dry flies a try. Often these conditions can be found along the edges of large midstream gravel bars on big rivers such as the Nushagak and the Togiak.

One of the most effective techniques is one that is a dry fly steelheading standard. Cast across and slightly downstream, keep a tight, controlled line, and let the fly begin to drag slightly as it drifts, creating a wake. This waking-dry-fly technique may bring about strikes anytime during the drift, but most often they occur right at the apex of the drift.

When you begin to get silvers up on top, it will become readily apparent that the fly pattern is not very important. All of the dry flies that I previously mentioned will work, and there are probably many others that would also work. It is my opinion that the silver salmon are more interested in the wake or disturbance that the fly creates than in the fly itself.

Catching silver salmon on a dry fly in Alaska is not a common occurrence, even in the areas that get a great number of returning fish every year. The biggest reason for this is that dry fly fishing for silvers is not tried too often. Some flyfishers have tried it under poor conditions, or they have tried it for only a couple of casts and decided it doesn't work. It won't work all of the time, but if you find silvers in low, clear water with a flat surface, it's worth giving a dry fly a workout for an hour. Once a silver does shatter the surface in pursuit of your fly, I guarantee that you'll begin to search for additional places to give dry flies a try.

Regardless of the technique or the fly pattern used, there is one axiom that is as close as you can get to being universal throughout Alaska: the earlier in the day that you fish the better your chances are at drawing strikes from silver salmon. In fact there are some guides who have it even further narrowed down. They'll tell you that the first three hours of daylight are the absolute best when it comes to fishing for silver salmon. I haven't kept detailed enough records to definitively say this is true, but I'm still inclined to agree with them. I've caught silvers throughout the daylight hours, but in retrospect, some of my highest catch rates have occurred during the early morning.

Equipment for Silvers

I prefer to use my eight-weight rod when pursuing silver salmon. My tippet strengths are usually in the eight- to 12-pound range, and my leader lengths stretch from seven to nine feet when I'm using a floating line. As with any other outfit for Alaskan salmon fishing, it doesn't make any sense to go out with only a single line. You will always increase your chances of success by carrying lines with different sink rates in addition to a full floating line. Leaders of about four feet are appropriate when you are using any of the sink-tip lines.

Reels should be able to hold your line plus 100 yards of 20-pound backing. Some flyfishers rely on the drag system within the reel while others prefer to palm the exposed rim of the spool to control the drag. Either will work, but if you choose to rely on the drag within the reel, make sure it is smooth. Any uneven tension when a silver salmon makes a quick run could result in a broken tippet.

Many flyfishers consider the silver salmon to be, pound for pound, Alaska's toughest salmon. There is no doubt that they do spend a lot of time in the air, and they are very receptive to flies. But are they the toughest? I recommend that you spend some time catching all of Alaska's salmon species and then decide for yourself.

EGL-SUCKING LEECH

Chapter 7
Rainbow Trout

There's little doubt that the rainbow is Alaska's number one draw for flyfishers. They are pursued wherever they occur, and the zenith of a flyfisher's trip here often occurs when that dream-sized rainbow slices into the air with an artificial fly stuck in the corner of its jaw. A flyfisher visiting Alaska may catch many rainbow trout, but often there is one particular fish that becomes permanently scorched into his or her memory. This fish is often the biggest rainbow of the trip, and in many cases it may be the largest rainbow trout the person has ever caught.

I've been very fortunate. On many occasions I have caught and released very large rainbow trout. I remember them all, some more than others. However, some of my more memorable rainbow trout excursions didn't include the giant rainbows that everyone pictures when Alaska is mentioned. Instead, my most vivid memories are of the days when it seemed that I could do no wrong, and there was a hungry rainbow behind every rock. One day in particular stands out.

A slate-gray sky and a steady drizzle combined to make looking into the water very difficult. The hip-deep water of this small Bristol Bay stream often made for excellent sight fishing for rainbows, but I had hit it wrong. The light conditions were bad and heavy rains the previous three days had washed out the few sockeye salmon that should have been lingering there on this early September day. I couldn't see any rainbows, and there was a good chance, with the salmon being gone, that the rainbows had left the stream in favor of the lake into which it flowed.

I tied on a size 4 Black Woolhead Sculpin and cast it straight downstream just to get the kinks out of my line and my casting arm. The fly, as so often happens with a big fluffy pattern that has not yet soaked up water, floated on top instead of sinking. It floated a few feet while I was busy adjusting the hemostats on my vest. I heard and saw the swirl at the same instant. Reflexes took over, and I pulled back hard enough to set a 4/0 barb into the mouth of a tarpon. Obviously, I never saw that fish.

Several different sculpin patterns produced some fine, fat rainbow trout over the next couple of hours. None were huge, but there were lots of them, and there was one that I'm sure would have tipped the scales at six pounds. A decent fish anywhere. I glanced at my watch and realized that a lot more of the day had gone by than I'd thought. The floatplane would be at the mouth of the stream to pick me up in less than three hours.

At that point, I saw my first rainbow of the day—the first that wasn't attached to my line, that is. It was holding about four feet away from the bank in fast but shallow water. The water couldn't have been more than 18 inches deep. The floating sculpin and the swirl of the day's first rainbow flashed through my mind while I reached for my box of dry flies. That rainbow took my Black Humpy on the first drift. It tail-walked upstream, cartwheeled downstream, and did everything else in its power to get rid of that fly. But I lucked out, and several minutes later I was releasing that wild, heavily-spotted beauty.

Rainbow trout. Duane Marler.

The poor light conditions persisted, and when the plane arrived, I had not spotted any more fish in the water, even in the shallows. Yet the rainbows had continued to rise freely to my dry flies. Lots of rainbows, maybe even more than were fooled by the sculpin imitations, plucked that dry fly off the surface even though there was very little insect activity. If only I'd paid more attention to that first cast!

I now try dry flies whenever I'm fishing for rainbow trout, no matter what the conditions are. The results have been varied and inconsistent, but there have been a few times

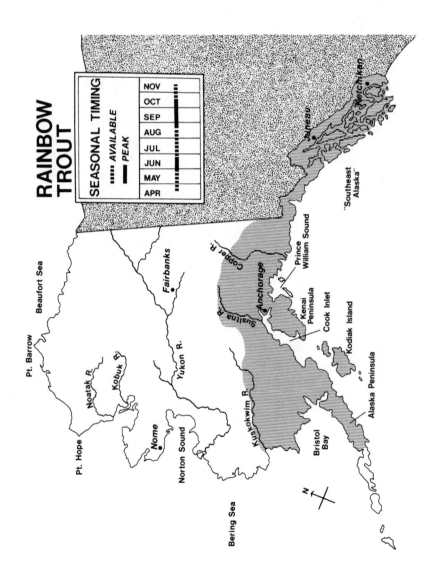

RAINBOW TROUT

SEASONAL TIMING

■■■ AVAILABLE
▬▬ PEAK

| NOV |
| OCT |
| SEP |
| AUG |
| JUL |
| JUN |
| MAY |
| APR |

when even a half-hearted attempt with a dry resulted in a fabulous day of fishing.

Every flyfisher is familiar with the physical appearance of the rainbow trout *(Oncorhynchus mykiss)*. Even if you don't live in an area that has rainbow trout, you probably aren't able to walk by a newsstand without seeing a photo of a rainbow trout on a fishing magazine. After all, rainbow trout are one of the most, if not *the* most, eagerly pursued sport fish in North America. Wherever you find the reddish side band and black spots of the rainbow trout, there's a good chance you'll find a flyfisher lurking somewhere nearby.

As is true anywhere else they're found, Alaska's rainbow trout exhibit a wide range of coloration. The size of the fish, its sexual condition, and even the location of the stream or lake in which it lives accounts for these variations in color. The color of rainbow trout ranges from silvery lake fish with very few black spots to brilliantly-colored fish caught from a river in fall. In some areas these river fish have a rose red band that extends from the gill cover to the base of the tail. The overall body color may range from dark to bright olive on top to a white or grayish belly. The amount and size of the black spots is also highly variable, and in some rivers in Alaska, the rainbows may have spots all the way down to the belly and on every fin. In general, the rainbow trout's coloration becomes more brilliant as the time to spawn draws near.

Their size is also highly variable, but it would be safe to say that the average Alaskan rainbow trout weighs somewhere between two and four pounds. Of course, there are some places where the average fish will be larger. In these areas, some Bristol Bay drainages for instance, the flyfisher stands a very good chance of hooking into rainbow trout that will exceed 10 or even 15 pounds.

Rainbows: Where and When

Rainbow trout are widely distributed throughout the southern portion of Alaska. They are also found in streams and lakes of the Southeast and on up the coast to the upper tributaries of the Copper River. Farther west, they are present on Kodiak Island, the Kenai Peninsula, and throughout the entire Susitna River drainage of upper Cook Inlet. In western Alaska the rainbow trout ranges from Port Moller on the Alaska Peninsula in the south, northward to the lower tributaries of the Kuskokwim River. They are not native to any areas of the interior or Arctic Alaska, but they have been introduced to lakes and at least one stream in the area surrounding Fairbanks.

If you start adding up all the square miles where rainbow trout can be found in Alaska, you will come up with a fairly large figure, but the premier region is Bristol Bay. It is here that anglers travel from around the world to fish for rainbow trout. Even resident Alaskans will get that faraway look in their eyes and an uncontrollable twitch in their casting arm when some of the fabled waters of this flyfisher's rainbow trout heaven are mentioned.

Some of the waters are legendary, but others are not so well known. Among those who have fished the area, the names of these waters will bring vivid memories and a strong desire to hop into a floatplane in search of rainbow trout. A few of the famous waters are: the Brooks River, the Kvichak River, the Copper River, Talarik Creek, and the Agulukpak River. In these rivers you stand not only a good chance of catching many rainbows, but the chance to hook into a really large specimen, one that could grace the cover of a national publication. The famous rivers aren't the only trout waters of Bristol Bay. There are others, many, in fact, that may rival at certain times of the year the more well-known places in terms of numbers and the size of fish caught.

Although Bristol Bay has an outstanding reputation for its rainbow trout, and rightly so, there are plenty of other areas within Alaska to pursue rainbow trout. Upper Cook Inlet streams, such as the Talachulitna River and Lake Creek, offer some fine rainbow trout fishing throughout the summer and fall months. Farther south, the Kenai River on the Kenai Peninsula turns out some very large rainbows every season.

An Alaskan flyfishing opportunity that is not well publicized is lake fishing for rainbow trout. The residents of the Kenai Peninsula, Anchorage, and the Matanuska-Susitna Valley are fortunate to have hundreds of lakes practically at their doorsteps. In some of these lakes, a flyfisher can catch many foot-long rainbows in an afternoon's fishing. Other lakes, and there are a few new hot ones every year, will yield many fish over 20 inches. Only recently have the flyfishers in the area realized the potential of these lakes. Consequently, there has been a blossoming of float tubes on many lakes—something that was a relatively rare sight in Alaska ten years ago.

Rainbow trout are available to the flyfisher throughout the year in Alaska. In some areas they may be present year-round, while in other areas they may exhibit complex migratory patterns. These movements may be triggered by spawning requirements, the availability of a food source, the onset of winter or spring, or a combination of two or more of these factors. While it is generally agreed that the largest rainbow trout are caught in the fall after a summer of feeding on salmon roe, most outsiders are not aware of the spectacular fishing opportunities available during the rest of the season.

In late spring before the salmon arrive in freshwater, rainbows can be taken on dry flies, nymphs, and smolt imitations. At this time of year, the streams will not be packed with salmon, and that makes for some exciting fishing for very hungry rainbows that are not yet keyed into salmon eggs. By midsummer, salmon have entered freshwater in full force, and flyfishers switch to matching the salmon egg. In late summer and on through fall, flyfishers bring out their flesh flies which imitate pieces of decaying salmon flesh. Winter and very early spring are not times of fast action for flyfishers, but large rainbows can be taken from the Kenai River from October through April.

Just after breakup in many areas, large numbers of rainbow trout can be seen in clear, shallow water going through their spawning rituals. Most people are rather surprised to find groups of rainbow trout bunched together like the clusters of salmon seen during the spawning run. The fish are extremely susceptible to any type of fishing at this point, but fortunately access is relatively difficult at this time of year. Critical areas are also closed to fishing at this time.

The Life Cycle of Rainbows

Alaska's rainbow trout are spring spawners. In their range this can happen from mid-April to early June. Their

Lake fishing for rainbows.

spawning behavior is similar to other salmonids. The female selects a site in a riffle area of a stream to dig a redd and is courted by a male. The female repeatedly moves to the upstream edge of the redd, displacing gravel and extruding more eggs until her egg supply is depleted. It takes the eggs one to two months to become fully developed, and then it may require up to two more weeks for the alevins to completely absorb their egg sacs.

Once rainbows reach the alevin stage, the rest of their life history is not so straightforward. Genetic variations and environmental conditions take hold, and their movements vary greatly from drainage to drainage. Some will move upstream, others downstream, and some will migrate to lakes. The movements of the young rainbow trout are not a concern of the flyfisher in search of adult fish, and they don't often present as concentrated a food source as juvenile salmon do during their migration to the ocean.

Lake Fishing for Rainbows

Lake fishing for rainbow trout in Alaska can be incredible. Not only are there many lakes that contain dense populations of two-pound fish, but there are lakes that contain large rainbow trout, the largest that I've ever seen.

Alaskan lakes can be fished by a variety of methods. Because of shorelines that are often brushy or swampy, I prefer to get out on the water to fish lakes. A canoe or small boat is nice, but it is so easy to travel with a float tube that it winds up being the method that I use most. The tube and bicycle pump packs easily into a car, backpack, or plane, and with neoprene waders you can be quite comfortable in Alaska's lakes during the summer.

Often when flyfishers first venture to Alaskan lakes, they think that because they're in Alaska the fishing will be different than what they're used to in the Lower Forty-eight. The truth is that it is not a whole lot different. But telling people that and showing it to them are two different things, and it's always funny to see their eyes light up with a look of recognition when a dragonfly lands on the tip of their rod. Typically you don't have the major emergence of one insect that brings about selective feeding behavior common in other parts of the country, but the macro-invertebrate fauna is remarkably similar. General impressionistic patterns that are used elsewhere will work here.

Selective feeding does occasionally occur though, and with more and more flyfishers heading out to the readily-accessible lakes, there will undoubtedly be more reports of it. I have encountered a few situations where midges were scattered across a lake's surface and an emerger midge pattern was the only fly that worked. Usually it doesn't have to be an exact imitation, but size is important. If you're fishing with one hook size different from the natural, you will have noticeably poorer results than if you have an exact size match.

I carry one pattern specifically for these occasions. It is commonly called a Mosquito Larva. Regardless of its name, it does a good job of imitating most of the smaller midges in Alaska. My fly box contains them in sizes 14 through 20.

A sporadic caddis emergence may also cause the fish to become somewhat selective. Again, the fish usually seem to be concerned more with the size of the fly than the pattern. A tan-bodied Elk Hair Caddis of the correct size to match the natural will usually do the trick, even if the naturals are smoky gray in color. I do, though, tie them in several shades of brown in sizes 8 to 20, and in the smaller sizes, 16 through 20, I tie a charcoal-gray version.

On a couple of occasions, I've observed rainbows zero in on some small black beetles. These fish were the most highly selective, in terms of dry flies, that I have witnessed anywhere in Alaska. I have not run across this situation too often, but when I have, the fish will take nothing else. This little black beetle, a Chrysomelidae species, is found in close association with lily pads and can be easily matched with a size 16 or 18 Crowe Beetle. Now I always carry a few Crowe Beetles with me when I am fishing lakes in south-central Alaska.

There are enough damselflies and dragonflies in Alaska's lakes to warrant carrying imitations of the immature forms, too. Mayflies, as well as the midges and caddisflies already discussed, can also be important. Scuds are incredibly abundant in some south-central lakes, and their imitations almost always produce well if the naturals are present.

Leeches, however, are the workhorse flies for the Alaskan flyfisher in search of rainbow trout in lakes. Although there are many mohair and chenille patterns, the standard in Alaska is the Lake Leech, made entirely of marabou. The pattern is tied on a size 6, 8, or 10 hook with a 2x- or 3x-long shank. A marabou feather is tied in at the hook bend to create a tail roughly the same length as the hook shank. Then the remaining marabou is twisted to form a single strand and is wrapped forward to the eye of the hook to form the body. Effective colors are black, brown, olive, and purple. Not only is the leech pattern simple to tie and productive to fish, but it also does double duty. Depending upon the size and the color, it could be easily taken as a damselfly naiad or one of the swimming mayfly nymphs. No doubt this has a lot to do with its success.

Stream fishing for rainbows. Duane Marler.

Stream Fishing for Rainbows

Even though there is some excellent rainbow trout fishing to be had in Alaska's lakes, it is clearly the wish of the majority of flyfishers to fish moving water. Although the patterns may differ a little, and the rainbows are, on the average, bigger than in most places, flyfishing for rainbow trout in Alaska is essentially no different than fishing for them anywhere else. To be successful you have to be able to read the water and then present your fly in a natural manner to the fishiest-looking spots.

Seasonal changes in fly patterns occur just as they do anywhere else, except that in Alaska the seasonal changes are usually dictated by the salmon runs instead of the prevalent insect activity. Don't get the false impression, as many people do, that Alaska's streams are devoid of insects. There are plenty of them, enough in fact that my college entomology texts and microscope still get a very good workout during the off-season. However, of primary importance to rainbow trout is the life cycle of the salmon. So let's take a look at the salmon and rainbow trout relationship from a flyfisher's point of view.

Early season is a time of smolts. At this time of year, these juvenile salmon get the urge to head for the ocean, and the rainbows lie in wait to pick them off as they go by. It doesn't matter what kind of salmon frequent the stream, early in the season some age class of fish will be gathering and beginning its downstream migration. Take a good look around the stream you are fishing to get an idea of the correct size of the prevalent juvenile salmon, and then tie on an appropriately-sized smolt pattern. The one that I use most frequently is the Blue Smolt, size 4.

This is standard streamer fishing. Cover the water with quartering downstream drifts and strip-retrieve the fly. Often that's all that is needed for a hookup, but there are times when the rainbows seem to be overly susceptible to one particular type of retrieve, so it pays to vary your retrieve. Quick six-inch strips are usually what I find most effective, but there are times when a slow, foot-long pull will be the most productive.

Springtime is a time of nearly continuous daylight in many parts of Alaska, and it does have an effect on the fishing. The juvenile salmon migrating out have a tendency to move downstream in large groups during the hours that coincide with the lowest light levels. So while you can have action that lasts all day long, if you fish the twilight hours you will most certainly see increased activity. I've been on some upper Cook Inlet streams at twilight and have seen the wakes of big rainbows chasing salmon in shallow water that had been barren the entire day. Under these conditions you can assure yourself of hookups if you strip in your fly very fast when you see a wake from a fish anywhere near the fly. Nine out of 10 times the rainbow will turn, increase its speed, and then crash into your fly with open jaws.

From early spring until midsummer is also a good time to use an Alevin. This is especially true if the river that you are fishing has pink or chum salmon. These two salmon migrate to the ocean right after they leave the gravel and are better imitated by an Alevin than a smolt pattern. Alevin patterns are not very common, and there is a good chance that you will not find any in fly shops or catalogs. The one that I use has bead-chain eyes, a pearl Mylar tube body, and some orange marabou tied in at the throat position to simulate remnants of the yolk sac.

With summer comes the salmon, and for the flyfisher in search of rainbow trout, this means it is egg season. Now I realize that fishing an egg fly is not aesthetically pleasing to some people, but you *cannot* deny its effectiveness. If you can fish a nymph, then you can fish an egg. The technique is the same except that in many cases you will be fishing to visible fish. Salmon will spawn in some very shallow areas, and the rainbows will be right there with them.

When you're fishing behind spawning salmon, a single-egg fly is one of the most effective patterns that you can use. There are two major types, the Glo-Bug and the chenille egg. Glo-Bugs are very popular and are available in a myriad of colors, while the chenille egg is most commonly tied in pink and is known as the Iliamna Pinkie. Don't become preoccupied with all the available Glo-Bug colors, pick three—one pink, one orange, and one red. Do the same with the chenille eggs, and you'll be set. I have used both types of eggs, but I prefer the chenille eggs for the simple reason that I can put a few wraps of lead on the hook shank before I tie the fly.

To be successful you'll have to get your egg imitation to drift very close to the bottom. Rainbows will hold anywhere from two to 10 feet downstream from a group of salmon, and they'll be very close to the bottom. They rarely move up in the water column for an egg, so a deep presentation is very important. Also, you will be competing with a lot of real eggs, so your fly typically will have to come within six inches of a holding rainbow.

When you do spot a holding rainbow, take great care in getting yourself in the best possible position to present your egg fly. When fishing with an egg imitation, more so than any other type of fishing, your first drift has the best chance of drawing a strike. Make it good. If the rainbow moves toward your fly only to pull away at the last instant, give it a five-minute rest and then try an egg of a different size or color. Too many casts with an egg fly without a strike will often do nothing but put the fish down.

If a rainbow does go for the first egg you present and you feel the resistance of the fish but fail to set the hook, don't waste too many more casts on that particular fish. I've often found that once a rainbow has been stuck with an egg, it's a lost cause for the next half hour or so. Go ahead and try another cast or two, but with no response, move on. When you're fishing a stream filled with rainbow trout it doesn't make sense to spend too much time with a fish that, in all likelihood, has been spooked. If it's a real large fish, mark the spot and come back to it later.

As I said earlier, fishing an egg pattern is very similar to fishing a nymph. In fact, the only difference is that you'll be using an egg instead of a nymph. Some flyfishers use a sink-tip line and a short leader, while others prefer to use a floating line and a leader from seven- to 10-feet long with split shot and a strike indicator attached. Either method will work. The key here is to use whatever technique best suits you and the water conditions. Whenever possible, I prefer to use a floating line, a leader from seven to 10 feet long without a strike indicator, and a weighted chenille egg such as the Iliamna Pinkie. Sometimes I will resort to one of the other methods, but I am not fond of either split shot or strike indicators.

The egg season will last through the summer and into the fall depending upon what type of salmon are around and how late they're running. In fact, you can successfully fish eggs right up until wintertime, because even after the spawning salmon are gone, eggs will continue to get washed out of the gravel. Many of these late-season eggs will have begun to decompose if they haven't been fertilized or if they have been attacked by fungus or bacteria. Consequently these eggs will no longer be orange but instead turn a whitish-yellow or cream color. The flyfisher who fishes the late season with an egg pattern will often do better with one of these colors.

In an effort to find out exactly what color egg the trout prefer at any given time, some flyfishers use a dropper so that they can work two different colors at the same time. I've used droppers for years; not only with egg imitations but with nymphs and wet flies as well. I should point out, though, that according to the latest interpretations of the state fishing regulations, fishing with more than one fly at a time is not legal in flyfishing-only waters.

Late summer also brings about the death of the salmon. Rainbow trout feed upon their decomposing bodies. Flies that imitate pieces of flesh are collectively called flesh flies, and they can produce some of the biggest rainbow trout of the season. Flies such as the Ginger Bunny Fly and the White Woolly Bugger are excellent choices at this time of year. Weight them and tie them in sizes 2 through 6 on 3x-long hooks.

Fishing a flesh fly is a simple matter. Use a weighted pattern and get the longest dead drift possible through likely-looking holding water. Takes will often be subtle, and here again, the flyfisher who is adept at nymphing will have good success.

Rainbow trout. Duane Marler.

Many dead salmon wind up high and dry on the stream-bank after they die. These salmon, like any other animal carcass, can become infested with maggots as they deteriorate. If this happens and then a fairly heavy rain occurs, the maggots will get washed into the stream. The effect is like chumming for rainbows with live bait. It's not an event you can count on, but if it does, and you're armed with a couple of size 10 or 12, cream-colored caddis larva patterns, hang on to your rod. Your arms will be tired of fighting fish before the day's end.

Salmon are not always the main target of feeding rainbow trout. They are, though, the easiest food source for the flyfisher to recognize, and consequently, flies that imitate one of the stages of the salmon's life cycle are the most frequently used.

Fly Patterns for Rainbows

Other stream organisms are widespread throughout the rainbow trout's range in Alaska and are easily imitated by the flyfisher. Sculpins come to mind first. They are one of my favorite flies for large rainbow trout. They are found almost everywhere that rainbows are found and are present throughout the entire year. Patterns and sizes vary, but I like Wool-head Sculpins in sizes 2 and 4 in either black, olive, brown, or a mottled combination of two or three of these colors. I also occasionally use a Marabou Muddler and the standard Muddler Minnow. When I do use the Muddler Minnow, I like to fish it in the manner of a damp fly similar to the greased-line technique used for steelhead. At these times I'm not convinced that it is being taken for a sculpin, and it could probably be replaced with a Greased Liner, Katmai Slider, or some other damp steelhead fly with equal success.

Leeches are another great year around food source. Rabbit-strip leeches and Woolly Buggers are both good patterns to use. Tie them on size 4, 3x-long hooks in purple, brown, black, and olive. One notable exception to this color selection occurs in the Bristol Bay region. Some leeches there are whitish, almost translucent, in color, and an all-white leech will sometimes work very well in this area.

While we are on the subject of leeches, I can't fail to mention the Egg-Sucking Leech. Basically this is a purple Woolly Bugger with a pink chenille egg tied in at its head.

Typically tied on a size 4, 3x-long hook, this is one of the most popular patterns in all of Alaska, not only for rainbow trout, but for any species of fish.

Many aquatic insects are well represented in Alaska's streams and rivers, although in much of what is written about Alaska, they are overshadowed by the salmon egg hatch. Both midges and black flies are abundant, but generally they don't seem to be of interest to catchable-size fish. Very small rainbow trout and juvenile silver salmon are much more apt to target these small insects for food.

There are, of course, many other Diptera present in Alaska's waters, but most of the time they're of no consequence to the flyfisher. The only one of minor importance might be the crane flies. They are found in many streams, but often the larva are unavailable as a food source because of their habits. A skater or a spider used to imitate the adults will occasionally attract a rainbow's attention.

Mayflies are common, but again the mass emergences experienced on streams outside of Alaska are uncommon here. There is quite a variety of species, but the flyfisher can be successful with a minimal number of patterns. Almost any series of nymphs, such as the A.P. Nymphs or the Marabou Nymphs, will fish well. If I had to venture a guess, I would say that the Gold-Ribbed Hare's Ear nymph is the most popular, not only because of its reputation but also for its effectiveness. I stock all of my nymphs in sizes 8 through 16.

Frequently-used dry flies are impressionistic rather than realistic. Stream-bound rainbows are rarely selective when it comes to dry flies, and you usually do not have to reach much beyond a selection of Humpies or Wulffs to get some action, if you are going to get any at all. My selection of Humpies includes yellow, orange, black, and red in sizes 8 through 14. For Wulffs I stick with those same sizes in the White Wulff, Gray Wulff, and Royal Wulff. In slower water or where I think that the fish may be a bit more finicky, I'll switch to an Adams, Light Cahill, or a Black Gnat. I carry all three of these patterns in both traditional and parachute styles in sizes 10 through 18.

Blue-Winged Olives provide an exception to the impressionistic approach. I've witnessed fairly dense emergences of Blue-Winged Olives on streams from south-central Alaska westward to southwest Alaska during the month of September when specific imitations, tied on size 14 through 18 hooks, fared much better than the catch-all patterns.

Several small to medium-sized stoneflies are common and are occasionally found in enough numbers to warrant a dry fly imitation. When I have had the opportunity to use stonefly imitations, the downwing style of an Elk Hair Caddis usually does quite well. Brown and a brown with a golden cast are the most common colors, but there is at least one lime green species that hatches sporadically throughout the season from south-central Alaska to the Bristol Bay area. To imitate it I use very light-colored elk hair over a body of one part yellow and one part bright green dubbing. No specific nymphs are needed other than the ones also used as mayfly imitations.

Caddisflies are the most common and diverse insect group of importance to rainbow trout throughout their range in Alaska. Again, mass emergences aren't too common, but adult caddisflies can almost always be seen fluttering on or near the water during any part of the season. Larval caddis imitations will fool fish some of the time, but mayfly or stonefly nymphs usually work better even if caddis are more abundant. This is probably due to the habits of the immature caddis that make them less susceptible to predation. Alaska does have members of the caddisfly genus, *Rhyacophilia*, which are free-living. That is, they don't construct a case. Most of them are green, and consequently, green caddis larva imitations often perform well in the rocky-bottomed streams where they are found.

If you're fishing on top, Elk Hair Caddis in sizes 8 through 18 is the pattern to have. I have seen a few Alaskan flyfishers use a Goddard Caddis or Henryville Special, but nine times out of 10 they'll be using an Elk Hair Caddis. If a rainbow isn't going to take the Elk Hair Caddis, then it probably won't take any other surface caddis pattern.

Springtime, during the smolt migration, is when baitfish patterns are used most frequently, but throughout the rest of the season other streamer patterns can be used with good success. Small fish, whether they are whitefish or juvenile salmonids, are almost always present, and a streamer fly that

Rainbow trout.

imitates them is always a good bet. An olive or black Matuka streamer in size 2 or 4 is always a good fish finder, as are some of the more well-known patterns, such as the Gray Ghost and Spruce streamers. The Thunder Creek series of streamers fools quite a few rainbow trout, and they are good flies to try anytime.

Lastly, there is the much-heralded dry fly that imitates a mouse, vole, or lemming. These are big, bushy deer-hair creations, some replete with eyes, ears, whiskers, and tail. I don't think that the small additions to make them look more realistic make them any more effective. Regardless of the complexity or simplicity of the pattern, they work.

There really doesn't seem to be a best season for mouse patterns, but if I had to single out one part of the year, it would be late summer or early fall. The only way to see if a mouse pattern is going to work is to try it. Almost all of my success with mouse patterns has been in western Alaska with a few limited instances of success on the Kenai Peninsula. Patterns should be tied on very large hooks that are comparable to a size 2, Mustad stinger hook (Mustad

#37187). Rainbow trout inhale these flies, and if a smaller hook is used many fish may be unnecessarily injured.

Logic has it that when you're fishing a mouse pattern the edges of the stream are where you should direct your casts. A mouse pattern that hits the bank and then struggles very close to the shore may closely approximate what happens to a real mouse, but often this type of presentation does not bring about the most strikes. In almost all cases, rainbow trout will hit the mouse in midstream rather than when it is close to the bank. Furthermore, imparting life-like action to the mouse usually doesn't increase its effectiveness. In fact, a mouse that just hangs in the current (even if it becomes submerged) straight downstream on a tight line usually results in the most strikes. I know this does not make sense in terms of imitating the real thing, but it works.

One exception to this occurs when you are fishing back-water areas where there is very little current. Here you will have better luck if you cast the mouse close to the bank vegetation or obstructions, let it rest, and then slowly twitch it back to you. This is especially true when you have spotted rises, swirls, or other evidence that a fish is working the area. This situation most often occurs during the twilight hours and occasionally on a dark, cloudy day.

Purists may shudder, but you don't have to use a finely-tied deer creation when you're top water fishing for big rainbows. Poppers—those designed for panfish and bass—also work quite well. In fact, they have some definite advantages over deer hair bugs. They never get waterlogged and they are available in a wide array of shapes and colors.

Equipment for Rainbows

Nothing out of the ordinary is needed in the way of equipment for Alaska's rainbow trout. The rods that I use range from an eight-foot, five-weight to a nine-and-a-half foot, eight-weight. This may seem like an awfully wide range, but when you take into account the varying conditions and the size range of the fish, it really isn't. In the spring I might be fishing size 14 to 18 dry flies and nymphs to fish that average two pounds in a shallow, brushy stream that is no more than 30 feet wide. In the late fall I could be making 60-foot casts with a size 2 weighted Flesh Fly that needs to be drifted through pools that may be 10 feet or more in depth. Here the fish may average six pounds but could exceed 15. Differing conditions, the times of the season, and the size of the fish all have to be considered when you're selecting a rod.

The reel should at least strike up a pleasing balance with the rod. This balance between the rod and the reel is a very personal thing, and I'll leave that decision up to you. You should, however, select a reel that will hold the appropriate size of weight-forward line and 75 to 100 yards of backing. A smooth, dependable drag is nice but not absolutely necessary. As in most other fishing situations, I prefer to palm an exposed rim of the reel to add drag, rather than relying on the reel's drag, but you should use whichever you prefer.

A variety of line types is always useful to present a fly properly under the varying fishing conditions in Alaska. I carry a weight-forward floating line, a very fast-sinking 10-foot sink-tip line, and an equally fast-sinking 20-foot sink-tip line. At times I may try other lines for the sake of experimentation, but these three lines would get me through the rainbow season from start to finish.

The tippet strength of my leaders runs from about four pounds up to 10 pounds. Lengths range from four feet to about 10 feet. Occasionally conditions may require something longer than 10 feet, but this would be considered unusual for Alaskan flyfishing. Use short leaders, no longer than four feet, with subsurface lines, and use the longer leaders with your floating line.

Even if you're interested in just one species, the rainbow trout, fishing conditions will change throughout the season in Alaska, and they can vary tremendously from day to day, especially if you're covering a lot of territory via a float-plane. Never assume that the outfit you used successfully today will also be the best outfit for tomorrow. Be prepared to adapt at streamside. In every situation you should evaluate factors such as water depth, current velocity, types and sizes of flies most likely to be used, and average casting distance needed. Only after you have a complete overview of the situation will you be able to select an outfit that both pleases you and is suitable.

FRANK'S FLY

Chapter 8
Steelhead

The overnight low in Anchorage was 15 degrees, and darkness settled in at about five o'clock in the evening. November doesn't have the best weather for fishing in Alaska. However, there are other people out there who are just as crazy as I am, and on Friday afternoon two of us drove 240 miles, one way, to get in two very short days of fishing. Our destination, the Anchor River, lies just 16 miles north of the town of Homer, the place where the highway ends.

Through frequent calls to Homer and close monitoring of the state weather reports in the newspaper, we thought it might be the optimal weekend (optimal for November, that is). There hadn't been any precipitation in Homer the past week and the low temperatures at night hadn't dropped out of the teens. Daytime highs had consistently crawled into the mid-30s. Clouds were forecasted for the weekend, and as a result the daytime high might creep up to 40. Two weekends prior the water temperature had slipped to 37, and it was likely that it had fallen a few more notches since then. It wasn't the best temperature for catching steelhead, or probably any other fish, but you have to take what you can get. We knew this could very well be the last outing of the year, and it would be a long and dark winter before any open-water fishing once again became available.

It was after dark when we arrived, and even though we couldn't see the water from the old iron bridge, we both optimistically decided that the water conditions looked real good. Back at the Anchor River Inn we were greeted by several other Alaskan flyfishers who had strategically situated themselves throughout the best holding lies in the bar and the adjacent restaurant. "Holding lies" is a very appropriate term to use here, because I would be willing to bet that the conversations taking place were heavily salted with extremely creative bits of flyfishing fiction, if not outright lies. Often it is difficult to separate fact from fiction, but there was one thing that you could be absolutely sure of—more fish were caught that evening at the Inn than the following day on the stream.

The next morning we were ready to go before daybreak. This may sound impressive, but it's not too difficult to beat the sun up when it doesn't rise until eight o'clock. We didn't think that fishing the first hours of the morning was necessary for success, but we did want to be the first to fish through some of our favorite holes. The air temperature was somewhere in the high teens or low 20s. Iced guides were a problem, but because there was no wind to bite through our heavy clothing, we were actually quite pleased with the weather. The water was low and clear, and we didn't move a fish. By midmorning, slow moving rafts of slush were beginning to appear on the river's surface. With the passage of each mat of slush, our flyfishing season drew closer and closer to its end.

By noontime we decided to break for lunch. After lunch a quick survey showed that the ice floes were increasing, and we decided to begin the five-hour drive back to Anchorage. As unbelievable as it may seem, many of the flyfishers stayed on to fish the rest of the weekend even though the ice on the river prevented them from getting any kind of a decent drift.

October fishing for steelhead.

I didn't hear any reports of fish being caught, but many of the flyfishers did develop a new flyfishing technique. They found that by using a high-density sinking line they could cast onto one of the slush piles, and then by jerking sharply on the line, they could get it to slice through the slush. It sounds crazy, but the reason these flyfishers were enduring abysmal conditions was simple—steelhead breed fanaticism.

Of course not all steelhead fishing in Alaska is done under these conditions. There are times when the weather is quite pleasant, even well into the late season, and many fish can be caught in one day. But there are very few lodges or guides who specialize in steelhead. Because of this, information on the run timing and the locations of the numerous small but productive runs of steelhead throughout Alaska are not well known.

The Alaska record for steelhead is a whopping 42 pounds. But don't come to Alaska with your sights set on a steelhead trip that will be loaded with fish over 20 pounds. That record fish was an extreme anomaly. A 20-pound fish is a very large steelhead anywhere in Alaska, and most of the time the fish will only be half that size. The best part of Alaskan steelheading is not the size of the fish but the numbers that can be caught. Catching 10 fish per day, in the eight- to 10-pound range, is not at all uncommon.

Upon returning from saltwater, steelhead are as bright as polished chrome. The dorsal, adipose, and caudal fins will often have small black spots. The other fins may have a few spots or none at all. The steelhead's overall color becomes much more pronounced once the fish have spent some time in freshwater. A band, running from the tail to the head, will turn reddish pink, and sometimes even the entire gill plate will take on this rosy hue.

Steelhead: Where and When

There are many places to catch steelhead in Alaska, but undoubtedly the most well-used steelhead stream is the Anchor River. This in no way means that it has the largest run of fish or the biggest fish. It is not a big river, and at first glance you might wonder why it is the most heavily fished. Once you look at it from an Alaskan perspective, it is easy to see why it is so popular. It is one of the few streams containing steelhead that is accessible via the Alaskan highway system. Furthermore, if someone says they are heading down to fish the Anchor, it is very likely that they will also fish one of the other three steelhead streams in the area. The Anchor River, Deep Creek, Stariski Creek, and the Ninilchik River all transect the Sterling Highway within 25 miles of each other. These lower Kenai Peninsula streams offer the local diehards a place to extend their fishing season into

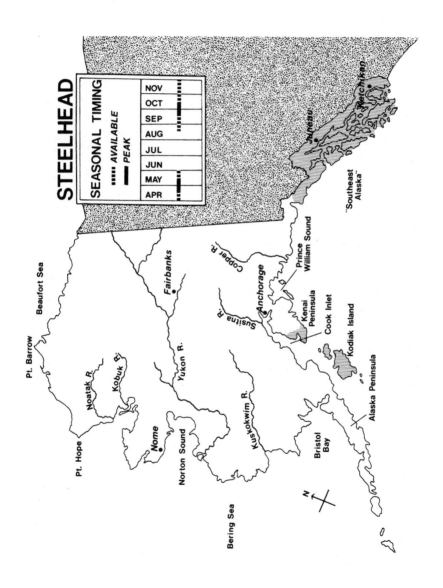

October and November, but I wouldn't recommend anyone making a trip to Alaska just to fish them.

Southeast Alaska is the place to go for steelhead, but outside of the prominent Situk River in Yakutat, flyfishers seem to know little about the runs. The rest of southeast Alaska, from Yakutat to Ketchikan, is a real sleeper when it comes to steelhead fishing. Although quite a bit of fishing goes on in the Southeast, most of it consists of saltwater trolling for salmon and bottom fishing for halibut. If you do a little investigative work you will quickly find that this part of Alaska is full of clearwater streams, and a large percentage of them support runs of steelhead.

So why isn't flyfishing for steelhead extremely popular in southeast Alaska? Well, first of all, most guiding services are keyed into salmon, and they are not even open during most of the steelhead season. The ones that are operating during the steelhead season are set up for salmon and halibut, and getting flyfishers to steelhead waters is neither a priority nor a regular practice, although this does seem to be changing, albeit slowly.

Well, then, the next logical step is to do it yourself, right? Sure, if you're willing to spend a lot of time getting to know one small area. Possible steelhead streams can be found almost anywhere among the maze of islands and channels. You will also have to be an excellent boatman, because major tidal changes can make once placid slots in between islands look like raging rivers. Also the weather, especially during the spring and fall steelhead season, is not renowned for being pleasant.

If at all possible, find someone who lives there or who has spend a lot of time there to take you out. At the present time, it's not easy to find good guides. I have known several anglers who have flown into different towns in the Southeast and were largely unsuccessful in finding a guide to take them steelhead fishing. But this should, and already is, beginning to change. Recently I talked with several guides and lodge personnel who are very interested in or are already extending their seasons by offering steelhead fishing.

If you do find yourself on a steelhead stream in southeast Alaska, the chances are very good that you'll have it all to yourself. The beautiful clearwater streams and the solitude make the time and effort that it takes to set up a Southeast steelhead trip well worth it.

I have spoken about the fantastic steelheading that southeast Alaska has to offer, but so far I have only mentioned one name, the Situk River. Where else would I send someone to fish? In deference to the wild steelhead of Alaska I usually try to be vague. Most of these streams are not the huge, brawling rivers that people commonly associate with steelhead. Many of them are quite small and easily waded, and they support small runs of wild fish. Because of this I don't think it is fair to single out one or two.

Let's take a look at Prince of Wales Island as an example of steelheading opportunities in southeast Alaska. Prince of Wales Island sits due west of Ketchikan, and along its approximately 150-mile length there are many short, rocky streams. Roughly three dozen of these streams are home to wild steelhead. Some of them receive modest fishing pressure while others rarely see any serious anglers. This is just one island, although it is a very large one, and it should give you a good idea of what the Southeast has to offer in terms of steelhead fishing.

A third area of Alaska where you can catch steelhead is Kodiak Island, better known for its bears, and its neighbor, Afognak Island. The Karluk River is the most well-known water and is usually considered to be the best spot to fish for steelhead on these two islands. As in the Southeast, a majority of these steelhead waters receive very little fishing pressure.

Autumn is the time to fish the waters of Kodiak Island and the Kenai Peninsula. Steelhead become available in mid-September, and depending upon the weather you could possibly fish for them into December. Mid- to late October is usually considered the peak fishing period.

In the Southeast there is both spring and fall steelhead fishing. Prime time in the spring centers around the end of April and the beginning of May, while late October is the best in the fall. In reality you could encounter good steelhead fishing anytime from October through May in the waters of southeast Alaska.

Regardless of when steelhead enter freshwater, they spawn in the spring because they are basically rainbow trout that live for a time in the ocean. Taxonomically speaking, they are both the same species, *Onchorhynchus mykiss*, but steelhead possess a trait which causes them to travel to the ocean. Usually after two years of stream dwelling, steelhead migrate to the sea. Their stay in saltwater may be as brief as a few months or as long as three or four years before they return to spawn.

Fly Patterns for Steelhead

If you want to initiate a really lively debate, start talking about fly patterns used for steelhead. There are many, some of which look strikingly similar, and everyone has a different opinion of them. You can fish Atlantic salmon hair-wing patterns, west coast originals, or large-sized trout flies. To complicate matters, you can find advocates for small flies (sizes 6 through 10) and proponents who favor larger sizes, sometimes as large as 1/0. To further confuse the issue, you can adhere to theories such as "dark day, dark fly" and "bright day, bright fly." Or you may have some faith in just the opposite.

Now I would love to be able to clear up all of this, but the truth is, I can't. Over a number of seasons I have pared down my Alaskan steelhead fly selection quite a bit. The flies I have selected are all very effective, but, and here's the dilemma, all of the old flies that I reinstate regularly seem to work just as well.

One particular afternoon I hooked two steelhead. One struck a size 4 Fall Favorite and the other took a size 4 Purple Woolly Bugger. You can't get much different than those two flies. So what does this mean in terms of Alaskan steelheading? You could presume that the flyfisher who has the widest assortment of flies has the best chance of success or that almost any fly will work if it is fished thoroughly by an experienced flyfisher. I suspect it is a combination of these two factors coupled with many other unknown variables.

Without unraveling the mystery of why a steelhead strikes at a particular fly, let's take a look at the flies that are used for steelhead in Alaska. Thinking traditionally, flies such as the Thor, Skykomish Sunrise, Skunk, Fall Favorite, and the Silver Hilton may come quickly to mind. And then of course, you could not leave out those other beautiful

North Coast creations such as the Comets, Bosses, and Optics. A lengthy list of these flies could be generated rather easily, and almost any flyfisher who perused it would surely make some deletions and additions.

Steelheaders are often without a game plan when it comes to fly selection. More often than not, they simply pick and choose patterns from a colorful fly bin or from a catalog. This does not mean that they will not catch fish, because patterns selected at random are often responsible for some spectacularly successful days astream. But from the limited amount of peeking into other Alaskan flyfishers' boxes that I have done, these traditional patterns (and I use traditional for lack of a better word) seem to have largely given way to more unconventional steelhead patterns.

Woolly Buggers take up a large share of the space in many Alaskan steelheaders' fly boxes. In a popularity contest, a Purple Woolly Bugger would probably come in first place, with its aberrant relative, the Egg-Sucking Leech, running a close second. All black, as well as olive-and-black and chartreuse-and-black color combinations, are also excellent choices. An all-orange Woolly Bugger and another Woolly Bugger-type of fly called the Battle Creek Special also account for quite a few steelhead.

Alaskan steelhead.

Everglow Flies and Krystal Bullets are also used in a wide variety of colors including orange, chartreuse, pink, red, and black. These are excellent patterns to try when the water is discolored from run-off. Because they are relatively new, these flies are not very well represented in the Alaskan steelheader's box, but in time they will probably garner more space.

Orange-colored flies are very popular in Alaska for almost all species of fish, and steelhead are no exception. Patterns such as the Polar Shrimp, the Babine Special, and the Copper and Orange are used because anglers assume, and probably rightly so, that the orange color represents the roe from salmon. Taking this assumption to heart, flyfishers have gone one step further, and instead of imitating just the color, they also mimic the shape of the eggs. Consequently, single-egg flies find their way into the steelheader's fly box in large numbers. Made of either yarn or chenille, they are tied in a myriad of colors. Another orange pattern that has a very good reputation among Alaskan steelheaders is Frank's Fly. It is neither an egg fly nor a standard steelhead pattern, but it has accounted for a lot of fish. It has an orange head, fluorescent orange chenille body, palmered orange hackle, and a white calf tail wing.

Non-attractor patterns are also quite effective for steelhead. Flies that imitate sculpins, such as the Woolhead and Whitlock Sculpins or the venerable Muddler Minnow, have always resulted in good steelhead action in Alaska's streams. Big stonefly nymphs, as large as size 2, also fool a number of steelhead. Logically speaking, this occurrence is a bit odd, because although Alaskan waters have plenty of stoneflies, there are not any species that even get close to that size. The largest stoneflies in Alaska are more closely matched with a size 8 hook. Whatever the reason, steelhead do take the larger versions especially when the water is low and clear. Flies designed to look like shrimp will also entice steelhead into striking. However illogical it may seem, these patterns often produce fish in stretches of water that are well upstream and far away from the shrimp's saltwater home.

What about dry flies for Alaskan steelhead? Once in late September a six-pound steelhead took my size 10 Hare's Ear wet fly that was dragging across the surface of the water leaving a wake in its path. Never before had I witnessed a steelhead rise to a dry in Alaska. Since that time I have fished dry flies over Alaskan steelhead with what can be considered only marginal success.

An unseasonably warm October produced the best results. In three days of fishing I managed to catch three steelhead on a dry fly. All of them struck a Katmai Slider. I must temper this achievement with the following caveats. The three other anglers who were fishing this lonely stream with me were almost all having double digit daily catch rates using subsurface flies, while I spent the entire three days fishing only a dry fly. The fact that I caught all three steelhead on a Katmai Slider isn't too relevant either. Although I did try other steelhead dry flies, I fished the Katmai Slider probably 80 percent or more of the time. In other words, I gave the fish little opportunity to strike other patterns.

As you might imagine, because of the extremely limited success I've had in my efforts so far, I don't see dry fly steelheading becoming a standard practice. However, who knows what lies ahead? In the future, a fly or technique may be developed that will have steelhead racing for the surface wherever they are found in Alaska. But I'm not holding my breath.

Tactics for Steelhead

Regardless of the tackle or type of fly used, there is a curious phenomenon that occurs on Alaska's steelhead waters. Some anglers always have some success regardless of the weather and water conditions, while others, more often than not, draw a big blank. I realize that the old saying—10 percent of the fishermen catch 90 percent of the fish—is probably true, but something different is occurring here. Some of the flyfishers that strike out are excellent anglers. They're definitely in the same league as those who are catching many fish. What's the difference? I am not positive, but I have a sneaking suspicion that many anglers, even very good ones, are fishing less than optimal water.

Experienced salmon anglers fall into an unconscious and completely logical trap—they fish salmon holding water

Alaskan steelhead.

instead of prime steelhead water. I don't want to make a blanket statement, such as salmon hold in pools and steelhead hold in runs, because either of the fish can be found anywhere in the stream. And of course there can always be a problem with semantics. Even among a group of biologists working under supposedly specific guidelines, there can be a lot of discussion about and latitude with terms such as riffle, run, and pool. Flyfishers are no different. Putting it into words is not easy, but in general terms, salmon do most often hold in pools and steelhead are most often found in faster runs.

On a heavily-fished stream like the Anchor River or the Situk River, it is not uncommon to see anglers walk right by classic steelhead runs and begin searching the depths of a big, slow pool. Sometimes they will hook a fish but not too often. What frequently happens is that an angler waiting to fish the pool will fish the faster water at the tailout and hook a steelhead. Hooking this fish will cause considerable attention, and other anglers with less than exemplary stream manners will crowd the spot and spook any other fish that may be there. Later, when the anglers disperse, they'll head upstream or downstream while searching the slow water of deep pools and will continue to bypass the type of water that yielded the previous steelhead. Old fishing habits, like some anglers, are difficult to change.

As I mentioned earlier, Alaska's steelhead streams are primarily small waters when compared with the bigger, well-known rivers of the Pacific coast such as the Skeena or Thompson rivers. Flyfishers familiar with these big waters will have to alter their fishing methods slightly. The classic swinging wet-fly technique is still the method of choice, but often the cast will be short, and a single reach of water can be fished from one spot. Lengthening your casts instead of taking a couple of steps downstream after each cast is a much easier way to fish these waters without disturbing the fish. In some instances, fishing for steelhead in Alaska is very similar to fishing pocket water for resident rainbows.

Cast straight across or downstream at an angle of up to 45 degrees. The object here is to get the fly to drift into a likely-looking spot in a natural manner. Keep your casts as short as possible so that you can follow your fly closely and control its drift. Concentration and a tight line are necessary to feel the soft take of a steelhead.

Equipment for Steelhead

With the proliferation of flyfishing equipment, it seems like there is specialty equipment for every situation, but steelhead tackle has always tended to be a little specialized. Steelheaders always fool around with their equipment to better suit the rivers they fish. For instance, very long rods and shooting heads are quite popular in many areas. It's not that you can't use this type of equipment in Alaska, because you can, but a 10-foot, nine-weight rod rigged with a shooting head is going to seem very out of place on a small Alaskan steelhead stream. Long casts are rarely necessary. In most instances, if you wade to a midstream gravel bar, a 40-foot cast is all you'll need to reach each bank.

A seven- or eight-weight rod is a good choice for Alaskan steelheading. Length is not too important because most of the streams are easily waded, and normally you can get to the best position to fish a productive-looking spot. As a result, there is very little need for line mending. Heavy-duty

Known as chinook, spring, tyee, or quinnat salmon in other places, they are called, simply, kings in Alaska. It is an appropriate name for a fish that, in terms of brute strength, is truly the king of Alaskan game fish. Chapter 2.

The next thing I knew, the king was at the tail of the pool, and it wasn't slowing down at all. Chapter 2.

With sockeyes ready to spawn clearly visible in the water, the fly-fisher's concentration turns to egg-seeking rainbows and char following behind. Chapter 3.

If someone tells you sockeye don't hit flies, just smile and say, "Yes, that's what I've been told." Chapter 3.

During a strong run of pink salmon, it's sometimes best to fish in sections of the stream that have less of them. That's right. Fish where there are fewer fish and you'll have better odds of catching them. Chapter 4.

Male chum salmon develop a conspicuous kype that is loaded with canine-looking teeth, but their common name, dog salmon, comes from native people's use of chum to feed their dog sled teams. Chapter 5.

Reckless abandon is an appropriate term for the silver salmon's over-all fighting style, which includes repeated runs at amazing speed punctuated by aerial cartwheels. Chapter 6.

The rainbow trout is Alaska's number one draw, and the zenith of a flyfisher's trip often occurs when that dream-sized rainbow slices into the tundra air with a fly stuck in its jaw. Chapter 7.

Rainbows and char have no trouble finding eggs from spawning salmon (and egg flies), even in glacial water. Chapter 1.

No matter where you are in Alaska, there's a chance there are some very good spots for char nearby. **Chapter 10.**

Flyfishers who've had the opportunity to catch Arctic grayling quickly learn one thing—the grayling is a flyfisher's fish. They can almost always be counted on to rise to a dry fly. **Chapter 12.**

Often the strike of a sheefish will be about as subtle as a swift kick to your shins. Nicknamed "tarpon of the tundra," sheefish are unique among Alaska's sport fish. Chapter 14.

reels that hold a lot of backing aren't necessary. During the fight, most steelhead will remain confined in a relatively small portion of the stream, seldom stretching out more than 75 yards of backing. Sophisticated drag systems are also not a necessity, and a reel with a dependable click drag mechanism that will prevent line overrun is adequate.

As always, it is beneficial to carry a range of line types. Some flyfishers prefer to use a floating line with a long leader. By using a weighted fly, they can adjust the length of the leader and the placement of the cast to get the fly to drift at the proper depth. Split shot can be added to the leader to get to even greater depths. When I'm fishing an area where the leader needs to be longer than 10 feet and split shot has to be attached, I prefer to switch to a sink-tip line. Leaders on sink-tip lines, of course, do not need to be long, and anything over four feet is usually not necessary.

Ten-pound test is a good starting point for tippet strength. Fish are seldom leader shy in Alaska, and there is rarely a need to fuss with tippet sizes. There is a need, though, to carefully consider your longer leaders, because it is sometimes difficult to get a size 4, weighted fly to turn over. If you build your own leaders, start with a butt section of at least 20 pounds and work your way down to a tippet of not less than eight pounds. The recipe I use for a standard nine-foot leader is roughly as follows: 40 inches of 25-pound, 30 inches of 20-pound, 20 inches of 15-pound, and 18 inches of 10-pound. I've used this leader recipe for a long time, but never before has there been such a wide choice of leader materials that vary so greatly in their ratio of breaking strength to diameter. Not only for steelhead, but for any type of fishing, it may be time to rethink or at least experiment with some of the new materials.

I think it could be said that flyfishing for steelhead in Alaska is still in its infancy. Alaskan steelhead waters are largely unexplored and unfished. This should be enough to get any steelheader frothing at the mouth and make him want to spend the extra time and effort it takes to find some of these sea-going rainbows of Alaska. If you're one of those flyfishers who does go the extra distance for wild steelhead, I trust you'll treat them with the respect they deserve and return them to the water.

LAMBUTH CANDLEFISH

Chapter 9
Cutthroat Trout

After a couple of minutes you begin to hear sounds that at first are too faint to recognize. There is so much to soak up the sound—lush undergrowth, moss-covered fallen trees, a full, light-filtering canopy, and a thick, soft sphagnum carpet. Even the staccato notes of a small, tiered waterfall are absorbed by the rain-soaked surroundings. The occasional grating, alarm-clock-like trill of the varied thrush is the only sound able to pierce the muted blanket.

The shrillness of the varied thrush's call makes you realize just how muffled the other sounds are. In the same way, the bright red and orange salmon berries make you aware that much of everything around you is green. The old man's beard hanging from the branches, the huge leaves of the devil's club, and the moss underfoot are all just one big blur of non-contrasting greens. In many places the creek, winding among the huge trunks of fallen trees and areas of dense foliage, is unseen as well as unheard.

Although this description fits most people's perception of a place like Washington's Olympic Peninsula, it also fits many of the valleys carrying streams that trickle toward the ocean on the islands of Alaska's southeast archipelago and on the nearby mainland. This land is covered by a temperate rain forest and in its creeks swim cutthroat trout. The fact that cutthroat trout are found here is quite fitting, because neither rain forests nor cutthroat trout are typically associated with Alaska.

My first cast into the small stream resulted in an underwater flash of silver and the pleasing resistance of a cutthroat struggling at the end of the line. The fish gave a short but spirited fight before I could draw it close enough to remove the fly. The second, fourth, and fifth casts into the same pool yielded the same result—scrappy cutthroat trout. For the rest of the morning it seemed all too easy to move from pool to pool and catch 10- to 14-inch cutthroats. Presented with a variety of small wet flies and streamers, the cutthroat showed little selectivity and lived up to their reputation of not being too difficult to catch.

Cutthroat trout (*Oncorhynchus clarki*) are found all over southeast Alaska, and they range northward to a few areas in Prince William Sound. Wherever they are able, they will venture into saltwater to feed during the summer months. Like rainbow trout, they also fare quite well in lakes that do not have outlets to the ocean. As you can see, variety is a major component of cutthroat trout fishing. Depending upon the time of year, a flyfisher may take them on a dry fly in a bog pond, on a swinging wet fly in a coastal stream, or with a streamer pattern in saltwater. This last method is perhaps the most interesting way to catch them.

For whatever reason, many anglers maintain an indifferent attitude toward cutthroat trout. I'm not sure why, but it can't stem from their physical appearance. Stream fish have a red throat slash and are covered with a liberal dose of black spots from head to tail. Even the dorsal, pectoral, and anal fins are spotted. Because of their varied habitat, cutthroats exhibit a wide range of coloration. The stream dweller is usually intermediately colored, falling somewhere between the silvery-blue fish of the salt and the dark, richly-spotted

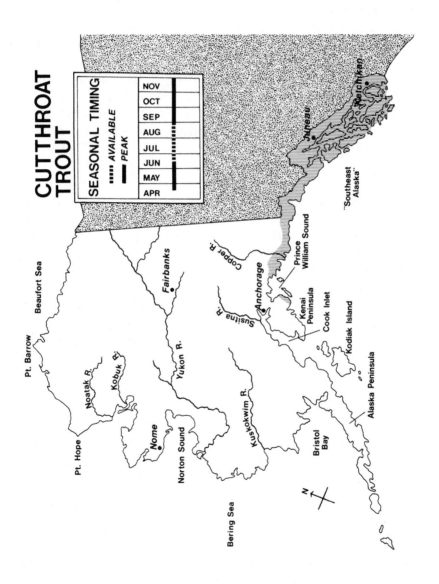

CUTTHROAT
TROUT

SEASONAL TIMING

▪▪▪▪ AVAILABLE
━━ PEAK

NOV	
OCT	
SEP	
AUG	
JUL	
JUN	
MAY	
APR	

fish of the bogs. These latter fish, depending upon the water chemistry and their diet, may develop an olive or bronze cast and sport the most brilliant red throat slash of any of the color forms.

Cutthroat trout are generally not difficult to catch. Some people would say that it is actually quite easy to catch them, and their unusual degree of willingness to strike a fly has often been ascribed to a fatal curiosity. From my experience, I'd have to agree with these sentiments, but I would be quick to add that the trouble can be finding cutthroats, not catching them. To find them you will have to know a little about their life history.

The Life Cycle of Cutthroats

By June, cutthroat fry have begun to emerge from the stream bottom. They spend the rest of the summer feeding in preparation for the lean winter they'll spend not far from where they emerged. Some of the two- and three-year-old fish, as well as the post-spawn adults, head downstream to enter saltwater instead of spending the summer in freshwater. This migration takes place from late May through early June, and they may stay in saltwater anywhere from two weeks to five months. Once in the ocean, cutthroats usually do not travel far from the mouth of their home stream, but some tagged specimens have been recaptured as far as 40 miles away.

After fattening themselves on candlefish, shrimp, and juvenile salmon, cutthroats re-enter their natal streams. The peak of this return migration usually occurs around mid-September. They overwinter in freshwater, and then sometime between April and mid-May, the female looks for appropriate gravel to construct a redd.

The average-sized 15-inch female deposits approximately 1,000 eggs in the redd she has constructed while a male fins alongside her to fertilize them. She then moves upstream and begins digging again which helps to cover the eggs immediately downstream. With the spring melt, the fish that have spawned return to saltwater and shortly afterwards the fry emerge from the gravel to once again initiate the cycle.

Cutthroats in Saltwater

Owing to the fact that cutthroat trout stay fairly close to home once they have entered saltwater, it seems logical that they would be easy to find. Originally this is what I thought, but I've had ample opportunity to change my mind.

Once while exploring some coastline during the month of May, I was about to pass very close to the mouth of a stream that I had been told contained cutthroats. After a short detour, the bay into which that stream entered was directly in front of me. The tide was coming in so I beached the boat and ran the bowline well beyond the high tide mark, securing it to a tree. I picked up my eight-weight rod (not having anything lighter with me at the time) and walked toward the stream mouth. Many casts and several flies later, I had worked my way well upstream. The only result of my efforts was a silver salmon smolt that had somehow managed to open its jaws wide enough to impale itself on my size 6 Black Gnat Silver wet fly. Bushwhacking a little farther upstream, I realized the error of my ways. It was the end of May—the cutts should be in the bay, not in the stream.

The tide was very near high when I arrived back at the stream outlet. Casting from shore was futile because a large area had been flooded and a cast of 80 feet put the fly in only two feet of water. Poling the boat offshore, I positioned it so that I could cast back toward the shore over 10 to 15 feet of water. Cast number two was greeted with a vicious strike midway through the retrieve, and moments later I released a healthy, silvery, foot-long cutthroat trout. The relatively small fish caught on my stiff eight-and-a-half-foot graphite rod didn't make for great sport, but I continued casting and catching fish until an hour after the high tide.

Six days later I returned with a friend. I'd convinced him that we'd be able to catch cutts on almost every cast. We gave our five-weight rods quite a casting workout, but the little bay was empty. If the cutthroats were there, we sure could not entice them to strike any of the flies that we pulled through the water. We fished the stream with the same results. We even explored the shoreline for a couple of miles in each direction until the tide had come and gone. I was dumbfounded, and my friend probably classified my secret cutthroat hot spot as just another fish story.

People knowledgeable in the ways of cutthroat trout in the salt do believe that they prefer shallow water and that they stay close to their home stream. Some say that cutts may commonly range as far as 50 miles, but most estimates are under 20, with a dozen miles as an average. With this kind of information, finding saltwater cutthroats may seem like an easy task. But if you look at the typical nook-and-cranny coastline of southeast Alaska you will realize that searching for cutts for 12 miles in both directions from a stream mouth is not as easy as first expected.

To complicate matters, they are usually found in dense concentrations, and they may be present in one cove but not in a similar one a couple of hundred yards away. So the

Saltwater flyfishing for cutthroats.

cardinal rule when hunting for cutthroats in saltwater is to find someone who already knows where they are and is willing to show you the spot. However, don't be surprised if they aren't there when you arrive.

Fly Patterns for Saltwater Cutthroats

When you do find cutthroats in saltwater, a Lambuth Candlefish is an excellent fly to tie on first. It is a standard Alaskan saltwater pattern and works well for cutts, although it is sometimes doubtful that they think it is a candlefish. Because the cutthroat's foray into saltwater coincides with an outpouring of young salmon into the ocean, they may mistake the Candlefish for a salmon smolt. The same bays that cutts spend time feeding in will often contain lots of salmon smolt, and there are a variety of silver-bodied baitfish patterns that can be very effective.

The Alaskan Smolt, the Blue Smolt, the Coho Spectrum, and the Coronation are just a few of the smolt flies that are regularly tied by Alaskan flyfishers, and they will all work for cutthroats in saltwater. In fact, many of the smolt patterns are so similar in appearance that it is doubtful that there would be a time where one would produce and the others would not. While it is always a good idea to imitate as closely as possible the natural forage fish, it is usually not necessary when fishing for cutthroats. Streamers that are strictly attractors, such as the Yellow Marabou and the Mickey Finn, will often produce just as many cutthroats as more realistic patterns.

Even though cutthroat trout may not be moving in and out of the saltwater with the tides, the productive fishing times are definitely influenced by the tides. The period from about three hours prior to, right up until the high tide usually produces the fastest fishing action. The hours of the day that coincide with this tidal stage seem to have little effect, if any at all, on feeding cutthroat trout. Nighttime darkness may have some effect on them, but during the summer when the cutts are in the salt, the Alaskan days are quite long. It is easy to put in a 12 or 14 hour day without ever seeing a sunrise or a sunset. Because of this, I have never made it a point to seek out an incoming tide after dark to try for cutthroats.

Equipment for Saltwater Cutthroats

Due to the nature of the small bays and coves where cut-throat trout spend most of their time in saltwater, it is often possible to get out of the prevailing breeze or at least position yourself so that casting can be comfortable. A five- or six-weight rod is an excellent choice to use in these protected areas, and it will complement the size of the fish nicely. However, anytime a flyfisher is close to the ocean, the wind is a concern, and you may have to call upon your seven- or eight-weight outfit. These are naturally not the tools of choice for fish that rarely exceed 18 inches, but they may be needed when the wind kicks up.

I prefer to use a floating line when fishing the coastal shallows. Typical cutthroat trout water will be 15-feet deep or less, and even if they are holding toward the deeper end of the range, they will usually move upward for the fly. Dredging the bottom rarely increases the number of hookups and quite often it does just the opposite. A floating line with a nine- to 12-foot leader gives you the flexibility to fish different depths on successive casts. Casting straight out from the beach, you can let your fly settle for a while for a deep retrieve. Casting in an arc pattern until you are throwing your fly almost parallel to the beach—right across the stream mouth if you are close enough to it—is a good practice to follow. Here you can begin stripping your fly in just as it hits the water and retrieve it at much shallower depths to prevent hangups.

The way a fly is tied also affects the depth at which it is fished. By tying a single pattern in weighted and unweighted versions and in differing degrees of fullness, you'll have the option of picking a bushy fly for shallow-water running, a sparser fly for a fast sink rate, and a weighted fly for a very deep presentation. Of course, I still wouldn't be out there without a composite line that has 10 feet of extra-fast sinking line at its tip. When there is a lot of wave action, any fly attached to a floating line will ride very close to the surface. Under these conditions, the sink-tip line may be needed to fish even fairly shallow water.

Cutthroats in Freshwater

While coastal cutts can be fished for in saltwater, most of the year they are also found in freshwater, and any flyfisher who searches them out will find that they have an uncommon attraction to flies. They are rarely finicky, and only rudimentary skills are needed to catch them. A simple swinging wet fly is usually all that is needed to bring results. Flyfishers in Alaska who have done quite a bit of stream cutthroat fishing will rarely use more than three or four passes of the fly through a pool before moving on to new water. The reason for this is twofold. First, the typical cutthroat stream is rather small, and a couple of casts will easily cover a small pool. Second, they are fishing under the premise that if a cutthroat is there and it sees the fly, it will take it. Imparting action to the fly as it drifts or strip-retrieving the fly after it has completed its swing may help bring about strikes, but even without these techniques, plenty of cutts will come to the fly.

You might have correctly inferred by now that fly selection is not of paramount importance when you are cutthroat trout fishing in Alaska's streams. This is the place to use some of the old-time wet fly patterns, especially those that

Typical cutthroat stream.

have a little flash to them. Roll casting a Silver Doctor, a Campbell's Fancy, or a Black Gnat Silver in a small stream is reminiscent of fishing for brook trout in New England or Michigan's Upper Peninsula. In fact, don't be surprised if you do catch a brook trout, because they were introduced into southeast Alaska from 1920 on into the 1950s.

Bright wet flies work well, and by fishing with them you are reliving a part of flyfishing's heritage. However, skilled nymph fishers, and less often the dry-fly fisher, can expect the same results as the wet-fly fisher. Here again, the particular pattern does not seem to be very important, and any impressionistic nymph, such as an A.P. Black or a Gold-Ribbed Hare's Ear in sizes 10 through 14, will work. A selection of dry flies does not have to be extensive, and almost any fly in sizes 12 through 16 will catch cutthroat trout.

There are also times of the year when cutthroats feed heavily on salmon roe. September is a prime month, and any southeastern stream that has a spawning run of silver salmon and a population of cutthroat trout is a candidate for this occurrence. There are a number of egg flies and egg-colored flies that will produce at this time, but if I had to choose just one, it would be a size 8 Iliamna Pinkie.

Cutthroats also inhabit stillwater that offers them no access to the sea. Once again the fishing is not difficult, and a four- or five-weight outfit with floating and sink-tip lines is all that is needed. Seven- to nine-foot leaders matched with the floating line and four-foot leaders on the sink-tip line will allow you to properly present a fly wherever the fish are feeding. Fly selection will depend upon the type of lake that you are fishing and what naturals are available, but with three subsurface patterns, a Lake Leech, a scud, and a damselfly naiad, you will have at least one pattern that will be effective.

The challenge of finding cutthroats and the beauty of the settings in which they are found make fishing for this species one of the unheralded pleasures of Alaskan flyfishing. Whether you pursue them in the quietness of a valley in the rain forest or from a boat along the Southeast's nook-and-cranny coastline, cutthroats are always worth the time spent fishing for them.

ALEVIN

Chapter 10
Arctic Char
and Dolly Varden

There is a small, clearwater stream on the Kenai Peninsula that is filled with Dolly Varden every August. It also has a heavy run of sockeye salmon, and this is, in part, why the Dolly Varden are there. The Dolly Varden move in behind the sockeye redds and gorge themselves on the roe that does not make it into the gravel, but this isn't the only reason they're there. At this time of year, they are beginning to show their spawning colors, and they too will spawn before leaving the stream to overwinter in deeper rivers and lakes.

When Dollies are set up behind salmon to feed on the roe, they are easily fooled by single-egg patterns, and they are fantastic sport on five-weight outfits. Thirty fish in one afternoon is not uncommon. Many of them weigh in at about two pounds, and one afternoon I landed one that stretched the tape at 28 inches. I was alone and didn't have a scale with me at the time, so I never did find out how much it weighed. That is just as well, I suppose, because now I am at liberty to be very gracious with my estimates of its weight.

The strike and the fight of that fish were typical of Dolly Varden and best can be described as solid. The take was fast and hard and resulted in unyielding pressure on the line. The fish had room to run, but instead it swam strongly downstream into a deep pool. From there it made its stand. Staying deep—Dolly Varden rarely jump—this fish gave me the impression that if I wanted it I would have to go and get it. Minutes that seemed like hours went by, but eventually I coerced the big male into some shallow slack water where I quickly measured it and started to revive it. Before I could get two hands on it, it splashed water into my face and shot back into the pool. My Iliamna Pinkie had lost all of its chenille and had been reduced to nothing more than a hook with a couple of wraps of lead. My leader was frayed, and my nerves were shot. This typifies what I like about Dolly Varden—they fight hard and never give up.

This little stream (it's not the only one; there are many others in the area that are very similar) does not see a lot of angling pressure even though it is relatively easy to get to by car. In August, most anglers are searching other waters for silver salmon or are trying to connect with an early steelhead. Dolly Varden just aren't one of those glorious, sought-after sport fish that people think of when they are in Alaska. Frequently I have difficulty finding someone to accompany me to this stream just to fish for Dollies, but when I do take someone, they are always very pleased with the fishing.

On one occasion, two flyfishers that I had taken there remarked that some of the fish looked like Arctic char. From the outward appearance of the fish, this could have easily been true. Some were silvery, while others had taken on a dark olive color with very bright spots along their sides and flanks.

Were these two different species of fish? The local experts told me no—these fish were definitely Dolly Varden, and the differences in coloration had to do with the time they'd been in the stream and their degree of sexual development. This sounded good to me. It seemed to verify the fact that earlier in the season there were more bright fish, and as the season progressed more of the fish darkened, and their spots became more vivid.

Following up on this, I found that there was quite a bit of contradictory fisheries literature about the Dolly Varden and the Arctic char. Species descriptions and range maps often did not agree. I continued reading, but it didn't help. The deeper I delved into the literature, the more confused I became.

To put it briefly, it became apparent that early on there had been confusion surrounding the taxonomic distinctions between the Dolly Varden (*Salvelinus malma*), the Arctic char (*Salvelinus alpinus*), and another species called the bull trout (*Salvelinus confluentus*). We have no bull trout in Alaska, so fortunately we need not worry about them. Problems with the distinction between the Dolly Varden and the Arctic char still continue. Although you can definitely distinguish the two by counting gill rakers and pyloric caeca, relying on outward appearances does not always give positive identification. This, coupled with the fact that Dolly Varden and Arctic char may be found in the same watershed, lets flyfishers call them whatever they want.

With this information as ammunition, I began to refer to all Dolly Varden and Arctic char as char, and a funny thing happened. Many flyfishers were suddenly eager to fish the little stream on the Kenai Peninsula because instead of catching Dolly Varden, they would be catching char—Arctic char, that is. Somewhere along the way Arctic char have become a more highly esteemed game fish than Dolly Varden. This is a dubious honor when you consider that both the Arctic char and the Dolly Varden have the same fighting characteristics and generally can't be distinguished from one another unless you're a biologist. No matter, flyfishers generally act indifferent when you mention Dolly Varden, but their eyes light up when you speak of Arctic char.

The Dolly Varden obtained its bad reputation early on in Alaska's history. At one time it was thought that Dolly Varden were capable of adversely affecting runs of salmon because of the number of juvenile salmon they fed on. In fact, during the 1920s and 1930s there was a bounty on Dolly Varden in the territory of Alaska. The bounty ranged from one-half cent to five cents for every Dolly Varden tail that was turned in to authorities. Evidently they gave little thought to the fact that Dolly Varden and salmon had coexisted for

Ten-pound char among sockeye.

many years without any interference from man. Subsequent study showed that many of the tails that bounties were paid on came from silver salmon and rainbow trout. Enlightened thinking eventually prevailed, and the bounty was terminated in 1941.

This doesn't explain why the Dolly Varden is still considered a second-class game fish when compared to the Arctic char. Maybe it has something to do with the name. Dolly Varden is a fine name, but it just doesn't evoke the images of clear streams in the far north that may be thought of in conjunction with the Arctic char. Regardless of your own predisposition, the two species are similar enough to be presented together in this book.

Informally, the Arctic char may be distinguished from the Dolly Varden by the pink to red spots that are present along its back and sides. These are usually larger than the pupil of the eye. Also, Arctic char may or may not have worm-like vermiculations on their backs. The Dolly Varden also has pink to red spots on its sides, but these are usually smaller than the pupil of the eye. Dollies will not have the worm-like vermiculations on their backs.

The overall body color of both species is quite variable, but it typically ranges from a dark brownish-olive to the silver sides of fish that have just entered freshwater from the ocean. The belly is usually pale gray or white except when breeding time draws near. The bellies of both the males and the females turn red or orange during the breeding season, with

ARCTIC
CHAR

SEASONAL TIMING

..... AVAILABLE
▬▬ PEAK

NOV	
OCT	
SEP	
AUG	
JUL	
JUN	
MAY	
APR	

the males developing the brightest colors of the two. The white leading edges of the pectoral, pelvic, and anal fins also become more brilliant at this time. In both species the intensity of the spots and the overall body color varies due to sexual maturity, size of the fish, and the specific locality in which they are found.

The Life Cycle of Char

Both Arctic char and Dolly Varden are fall spawners, and their spawning behavior is similar to that of other salmonids. The female selects a site to build the redd and is courted by one or more males. After depositing some of her eggs, she will continually move forward to deposit more, and at the same time the gravel that she displaces will cover the previously laid eggs. Dolly Varden construct their redds in riffle areas where fairly swift currents are present, while Arctic char prefer to spawn on gravel shoals in lakes. Because of their broad latitudinal range, spawning may take place anytime from late August through the month of November.

The life histories of the two species are quite different, and in fact, the Dolly Varden alone may exhibit one of several different behaviors depending on the type of habitat it occupies. For example, there are both northern and southern forms of an anadromous stream-dwelling Dolly Varden. There are also northern and southern forms of non-anadromous stream dwellers. Finally, there are Dollies present only in the southern form which live in stream/lake systems. Confused yet? Fortunately, the Arctic char presents a much simpler case. Throughout Alaska, Arctic char are confined to lake systems and are non-anadromous.

The sizes of these two fish vary greatly depending upon their specific life histories. The anadromous varieties of northern Dolly Varden normally attain the greatest size, even though Arctic char commonly live to a much older age. Although the Dolly Varden is found throughout Alaska, the largest specimens continually come from the Noatak and the nearby Wulik and Kivalina rivers. These fish often weigh in the vicinity of 10 to 15 pounds. In more southerly parts of their range, a five- or six-pound specimen of either species would be considered a very nice fish.

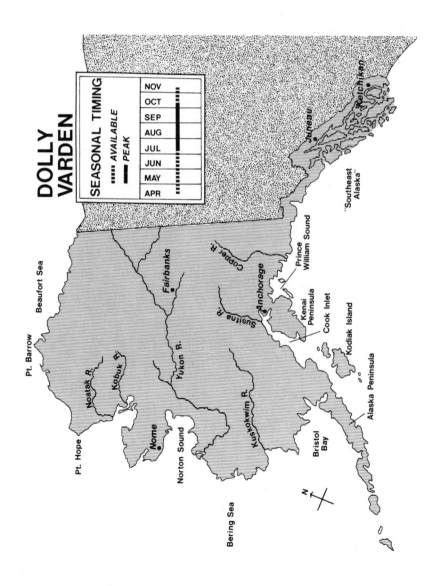

DOLLY VARDEN

SEASONAL TIMING

■ ■ ■ AVAILABLE

▬▬ PEAK

NOV	
OCT	
SEP	
AUG	
JUL	
JUN	
MAY	
APR	

Char: Where and When

Throughout the rest of Alaska, it's difficult to single out particular places for Arctic char or Dolly Varden fishing, because no matter where you are, there's a chance that there are some very good spots nearby. A few worth mentioning are the Togiak River, the Goodnews River, the Agulukpak River, and still farther east, the Iliamna River. From Kodiak Island to Prince William Sound and on down through southeast Alaska, there are hundreds of streams that have plenty of the anadromous variety of Dolly Varden.

Because of the similarities in the techniques, equipment, and flies used to catch them, I will from this point forward refer to both Arctic char and Dolly Varden collectively as char. Dolly Varden are sometimes referred to as trout, but technically they are char, not trout.

Seasonally there is no bad time to fish for char, but some times of the year are better than others. The first peak occurs somewhere between mid-June and early July. This coincides with the migration of smolt upon which the char feed heavily. During the latter months of summer, the adult salmon will play a bigger role in where and how char can be caught. Some char may remain within the depths of a lake, but many will follow salmon to their spawning grounds. Here they will feed on eggs that fail to make it into the redds. So, during the early season look for smolt and later on look for spawning salmon. In both cases you will find char somewhere nearby.

Fly Patterns for Char

There are many smolt patterns, but when I'm in an area that has heavy concentrations of smolt, I usually choose a size 4 Blue Smolt. My second choice would be a Coronation of the same size. Most often, though, char are not too finicky when they are slashing into schools of smolt, and there are many other patterns that will work just as well.

During periods of very low water or when the smolt aren't extremely abundant, I prefer to use sparser patterns. The Black-Nosed Dace and the Squirrel Hair Smolt are two patterns that I tie very sparse for these occasions. Also, the Thunder Creek flies will work very well under these conditions.

The Dace and the Squirrel Hair Smolt are best tied unweighted and in smaller sizes than the two previously mentioned patterns. Size 6 or 8, 3x-long hooks are a good choice.

June and July are excellent months to use an alevin imitation. Alevin patterns are not too common, and there is no real standard. However, they are very effective. The pattern that I have described in the fly appendix has always worked extremely well for me, especially just prior to and at the tail end of the smolt run. The two other patterns that I have had limited experience with, but with very promising results, are the Fry Fly and the Egg & I.

As the season progresses, Alaskan flyfishers begin reaching for their egg flies. There are many egg patterns, and as with rainbow trout fishing, Glo-Bugs are the most common. Chenille eggs, such as the Iliamna Pinkie, run a distant second in terms of popularity, but I still prefer them to Glo-Bugs. Char, unlike rainbows, have a tendency to take larger egg patterns. The double-egg flies, such as the Two-Egg Sperm Fly and the Babine Special, are very good char patterns. Carry them in sizes 2 through 6.

Topwater patterns are not often thought of when a flyfisher's intentions turn to char, but I have caught enough of them on dry flies now to believe it is not a fluke. I have had some fabulous days of fishing Humpies and Wulffs for char in Bristol Bay's Wood River system and on the Kenai Peninsula. In August and September, a light tan- or yellow-bodied Elk Hair Caddis will often bring a char to the surface. Undoubtedly more char could be enticed to the top, but flyfishers seldom throw dry flies at them. Instead they opt for subsurface patterns, which will often yield more fish. However, dries shouldn't be totally overlooked. In general, I use the same selection of dries for char as I use for rainbow trout.

As the salmon begin to die in late summer and early fall, flesh flies become very important. The standard patterns used to imitate pieces of flesh are the White Bunny Fly, the Ginger Bunny Fly, and the White Woolly Bugger. Another pattern that often escapes many flyfishers' attention is the Battle Creek Special. Arguably, this pattern is often considered more of an egg pattern than a flesh fly because of its pink chenille body, but there is a lot of similarly-colored

Lonely flyfishing for Dolly Varden.

salmon flesh in the streams, and the fly produces fish. Try this one and the other flesh patterns in sizes 2 through 6.

If you wanted to draw up a list of the most effective flies for char in Alaska, smolt-imitating flies and egg patterns would have to share the top spot. Nymphs might not even be listed. This poor showing is not indicative of how effective they are, but rather it is a mark of how seldom they are used. It is not uncommon for flyfishers to stand staunchly by their smolt patterns until the egg season rolls around. Sure, they'll catch fish, but during the lull between the time of frenzied smolt activity and the onset of spawning, nymphs will consistently take char. As a matter of fact, nymphs will often continue to take char after salmon eggs become available.

This happened to me on the Iliamna River several years ago. It was late August, and the water was packed with spawning sockeye salmon. Behind every redd I could see the dark shapes of char. Single-egg flies produced a few fish but not nearly as many as I thought I should be catching. I switched egg flies. I tried different colors, sizes, and styles, anything that could even remotely be considered an egg pattern. I caught a few fish, but quite often the char would move to intercept the fly and then at the last instant would turn away. In desperation I tied on a nymph, a size 12 A.P. Black. It worked like the single-egg fly should have—the char couldn't resist it.

At other times I have caught char on nymphs while spawning salmon were in the area, but that was the only time that I experienced a complete reversal from egg feeding to nymphing. I don't have an explanation for it, not even a good guess. However, if you are fishing single-egg flies for char and they show interest but balk just before the take, try a nymph. It may turn your day completely around.

I use the same nymphs that I use for rainbow trout—A.P. Nymphs, Marabou Nymphs, and the Gold-Ribbed Hare's Ear. I have also had some success with the Pheasant-Tail Nymph, the Flashabou Nymph, and the Zug Bug. I like the Flashabou and Pheasant Tail in sizes 12 and 14 and the Zug Bug in sizes 8 and 10.

Most of the other fly patterns that were mentioned in reference to rainbow trout will also work equally well for char. Sculpins, Woolly Buggers, and the Egg-Sucking Leech will all take char consistently. Also, brightly-colored flies, such as the Mickey Finn, are great to use for char. As a general rule, bright patterns are much more attractive to char than to rainbow trout. In this respect char are more like steelhead, and consequently they are often caught on flashy steelhead patterns that are not intended for them.

Capitalizing on a char's affinity for bright colors, many flyfishers employ a method called the attractor-yarn technique with great results when they're fishing for char. A brightly-colored piece of yarn is tied to the leader two feet ahead of a more somber offering, such as a nymph. The yarn should should sink with the fly, rather than float. Many times a char will move a great distance across a stream to inspect a bright object but will refuse it. The attractor yarn technique solves this problem, because the char is attracted to the bright yarn but sees the nymph and takes it for a meal.

This practice of adding a bit of colored yarn to the leader is used successfully for rainbow trout as well. It is also used by many flyfishers when fishing the grayish-green, glacial waters common in Alaska. Fishing techniques for those waters are described in Chapter 1.

Tactics for Char

Presenting your fly to char is not a difficult matter. Egg flies, flesh flies, nymphs, and dry flies are all best dead-drifted, but char are much more forgiving than rainbow trout. Often they will take a fly, especially a dry fly, after it has begun to drag. This is sometimes so true that an intentional mend to make your fly drag will increase the number of strikes. However, this is not always the case, and these patterns should be tried with a dead-drift first.

Char do react differently to smolt patterns, alevins, and attractor patterns such as the Mickey Finn or the Polar

Dolly Varden.

Shrimp, and these should be given some action. Stripping in some line as the fly drifts to give it a twitching or darting motion is a deadly tactic for char. The same technique works with Woolly Buggers and baitfish patterns—the more movement they have, the more strikes you will get. Throwing a belly into the line to make one of these flies zip across the current is often irresistible to char. Also, casting straight downstream and retrieving the fly in short, sharp strips is a good tactic.

Their propensity to hit a moving fly may have something to do with the type of water in which char can often be found. While they will move into swift water to feed on salmon eggs, they prefer deeper pools and the slowest water at inlets and outlets to pursue smolts and other baitfish. In these areas, they can often be seen in schools numbering 50 or more. Here they stay deep and attack their prey from below.

These heavy concentrations of char can be seen easily from the air while traveling by small plane. This is often a tactic used by guides and outfitters to find char. Once the char are spotted, the plane lands nearby, and the anglers usually find the fishing to be ridiculously easy. A fish on every cast is not unusual, and the fishing can actually become monotonous and boring for some anglers. This is often where the stories of four-pound fish on every cast originate. If you ever happen to hear a great Alaskan fish story of this type, listen closely. If the story is about char, there's a good chance the storytellers are not exaggerating.

The equipment needed to catch char is no different than that described for rainbow trout. In many cases you may catch char and rainbow trout on alternate casts because they may inhabit the same waters and respond to the same flies. When selecting your equipment, remember to size up the entire situation, keeping two important points in mind: the size of the flies that you'll be using and the average size of the fish that you'll be fishing for. This will act as your best guide as to what size outfit you should use.

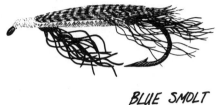

BLUE SMOLT

Chapter 11
Lake Trout

I've acquired some quality fishing gear over the years, but for a long time my five-weight rod, often referred to as "the noodle" by my friends, had been one of my weak spots. It seemed that no matter how much funding I stockpiled for equipment, there was always something more pressing than replacing my five-weight rod. Although others refer to it as a noodle, it's not a true noodle rod. It is an eight-foot graphite, and in deference to the manufacturer I will not mention the brand. (The rod is one of their early graphites and not the top of their line. Their present day rods are much better.)

This five-weight was one of my first graphite rods, and over time I amassed a wide assortment of reels, spools, and lines to go with it. Even though I now have other five-weight rods, the noodle remains my sentimental favorite. So it was not an unusual situation to find me bobbing on the surface of a backcountry lake in July with the noodle in hand. I'd figured that there would be midges all over the surface, and the noodle is a great rod to use with tiny flies and a floating line.

Chironomids turned out to be scarce and so did the normally ubiquitous caddis, but between the two of them, plus some terrestrial insects, the fish were rising sporadically. Just before sunset, the wind kicked up and the dry fly action slowed to a standstill. I noticed plenty of small whitefish milling around in the shallows, so I replaced my light tippet with a heavier one and knotted on a Black Ghost. The rainbows that I thought might be feeding on the whitefish didn't think too much of my offering, so I switched to a sink-tip line and tied on a heavily-weighted Woolly Bugger. Now with a weighted fly and a sink-tip line, casting with my little noodle is not a thing of beauty. In fact, it can be fairly dangerous. I enjoy casting, but the thought of that size 4 Woolly Bugger embedded in the back of my neck or, worse yet, in my float tube, made trolling seem like a very good idea, much better than casting.

I let the line sink, stripped out more line from the reel, and then paddled slowly along the shoreline over about 15 to 40 feet of water. The last particles of light were disappearing on the horizon, and a pair of loons did their best to keep the place from getting too quiet. In half an hour it would be midnight, but I wasn't worried about getting caught on the lake in total darkness. It would begin to get lighter before complete darkness had a chance to take over the skies. During the middle of summer in Alaska, the sun doesn't do a very good job of getting below the horizon.

My line hesitated a few times. A good sign, I thought. My fly must be cruising very close to the numerous deadfalls that stuck out from the shoreline. I stripped my line in to remove any debris that might have caught on the hook, but it was clean. I let the fly sink back into the depths and resumed a slow paddle. Moments later I detected another slight tap. I stopped paddling, gathered in the slack line and waited. I felt another faint tap which I greeted with a quick motion, lifting the rod up over my head. For the first second or two nothing moved—I though I'd hooked an inanimate object. But this thought didn't last long because my little noodle doubled over, and the racheting of my reel scared the pair of loons that had drifted unusually close.

Releasing a lake trout.

Line shot out through the guides, and I followed the fish to deeper water. It went well into my backing, but the strange thing was that it was going almost straight down. The fish stayed deep for a long time, and my little noodle strained to bring the fish to the surface. Eventually I wrestled the fish up, and I spun my float tube around to get a better look at it. It was a lake trout of about 23 inches.

I hadn't intended on catching lake trout. After all, it was July, and everybody knows that to catch lakers in the summer you have to troll very deep with exceptionally large

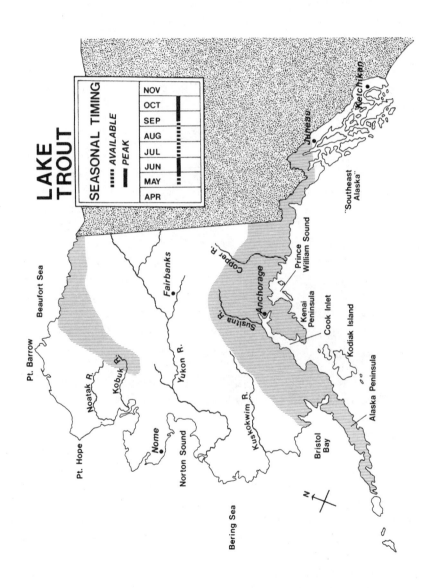

LAKE TROUT

SEASONAL TIMING

- ▪▪▪ *AVAILABLE*
- ▬ *PEAK*

NOV	
OCT	
SEP	
AUG	
JUL	
JUN	
MAY	
APR	

pieces of shiny metal. What a rare occurrence. I had just defied the odds and caught a lake trout at the wrong time of year with the wrong kind of gear. Imagine how I felt the next evening when I caught and released several more.

Since that time I have caught lake trout in Alaska during every month from May through October. Prior to this I had thought, as do many other flyfishers, that outside of two unusual periods in the spring and the fall, lake trout were for the most part outside the realm of flyfishing. Now I know different.

The lake trout (*Salvelinus namaycush*) is the largest member of the Salvelinus genus, which also includes the Arctic char and the Dolly Varden. It is easily recognized by its deeply-forked tail and its numerous white to yellowish markings, which are a blend of spots and vermiculations. These markings are never pink or red, and this fact quickly and easily separates lake trout from other char. The lake trout's overall background color varies from gray to dark green, and its belly is creamy white. The tail and dorsal fins are also spotted, while the pectoral and pelvic fins may be orange with a bright white anterior edging in some populations.

In the northern part of Alaska, lake trout can be found in the deeper lakes of the Arctic foothills. Southward, they are located through the Bristol Bay watershed to the Alaska Peninsula and eastward to the Kenai Peninsula and on to the northernmost part of southeast Alaska. The lake trout's occurrence within their range from north to south isn't continuous, and they are absent from large areas such as the lowland regions of the Yukon and Kuskokwim river valleys.

As much as their name may imply, lake trout are not strictly relegated to Alaska's lakes. Lakers frequently move back and forth between a lake and the flowing water that spills into and out of it. While these movements are generally of a short transitory nature, I have caught plenty of lake trout far enough away from their stillwater habitat to believe that some of their forays into running water are anything but quick trips. In some deep pools of a Kenai Peninsula stream where I often fish for Dolly Varden, I catch 10- to 15-inch lake trout with surprising regularity. There are also a number of rivers in southwest Alaska where more than once I stumbled upon decent fishing for lake trout at least 10 miles from the nearest lake. Above the Arctic Circle on the Kobuk River, I watched with amazement as a native family hauled in a seine that contained dozens of whitefish and grayling and one five-pound lake trout. The moral of all this, I guess, is don't rule out lake trout just because the water is moving.

Lake trout spawn in the fall over a clean, rocky lake bottom in water depths ranging from one to 100 feet. Due to its extreme geographical range, the lake trout's actual spawning period may occur anytime from as early as late August in the north up until November in the south. Although they have been reported to spawn at depths of 100 feet, they can be commonly found on shoals from four to 10 feet deep during the spawning period. The males usually precede the females to the spawning area by several days. Spawning takes place at night, so even after both sexes have arrived, they may be absent from the shoal at midday. They may spend their day in deeper waters away from the shoal, but they will begin to return by late afternoon. The eggs incubate anywhere from three to five months before hatching, and it will be approximately seven years before the fish return, sexually mature, to the fall spawning shoals.

Lake Trout in Fall

Fall is when the Alaskan hillsides are bright red with fireweed. The once green leaves of the willows are now yellow, and the tundra looks as though it should be on a watercolorist's easel. Condensation on the outside of the tent and the water in the coffee pot will have turned solid overnight. Wading shoes may have to be dipped into the water to make them pliable enough to put on and lace up. Once you do get them on, you can concentrate on getting the stove fired up so you can enjoy one of the most satisfying cups of coffee in the world. There may be a slight drizzle, a downpour, or it may be clear and crisp, but the weather will have little effect on the flyfishers who have their sights set on lake trout. Fall is the time to find lakers—big lakers—in the shallows.

Productive flies at this time of year have more to do with the whim of the angler than the fish. A whole host of attractor patterns will work, because the fish are very aggressive when they initially arrive near the spawning beds. Later, as the spawning actually begins, they are much less apt to strike any type of fly. During lakers' pre-spawn phase, bucktails of red and white, yellow and white, and blue and white, as well as patterns such as the venerable Mickey Finn, will all get strikes when they are stripped past these fish. Many of the attractor patterns designed for salmon will also work. The Flash Fly works very well, and the addition of Flashabou to any standard streamer pattern will increase its effectiveness.

To quietly wade the shallows or to row into a secluded cove and see lakers swimming around in less than 10 feet of water is quite startling. As the days begin to grow short and the surface temperatures cool, this is a common occurrence. Common enough, but difficult at best to predict exactly when and where it will happen. There are two main reasons for this: the fish may be in the shallows for as little as a week, and the spawning bed may be limited to a small area, even in a large lake.

So how do you go about finding fall hot spots for Alaskan lake trout? The best way is to go out with someone who already has located a good area and has at least a general idea of when the fish will be there. On your own, look for bays and coves that have rubble bottoms with water that is five to 15 feet deep. Offshore shoals may also fulfill the spawning requirements of lake trout. When to look for them is a less easily defined variable. Late August may be an appropriate time to search lakes of the interior and Arctic regions, but mid-October may be the best time in the Bristol Bay area.

The key, though, is to be aware that you have the opportunity to fish for lakers in the fall and that you don't let it pass. Even if you don't find them concentrated in the shallows, the water will have begun to cool, and they will at least be in the flyfisher's range. Fishing for other species such as rainbow trout and grayling is often excellent at this time of year, and fast action with these fish can fill the gaps in a two or three lake-trout day.

Many Alaskan outdoor enthusiasts will have turned to hunting at this point in the season and will not look at fishing equipment again until it is time to drill little holes in the ice. Of the few who do continue to fish, many have only steelhead on their minds, and they often overlook the fine fall fishing opportunities for lake trout. Even lakes accessible by roads will be devoid of anglers. There are many lakes along the Denali Highway that hold lake trout. Lake Louise off the Glenn Highway is a popular lake trout fishery, and Skilak Lake and Hidden Lake on the heavily-fished Kenai Peninsula contain lake trout. Because of this lack of fishing pressure, the best spots and exact times for lake trout are not well-known, but—and this is the best part—when you do find the fish, the chances are excellent that you'll have them all to yourself.

Lake Trout in Spring

Springtime on lake trout waters is also a time of excitement for flyfishers. As the ice recedes and in many cases

Float tube flyfishing for lakers.

before it is gone completely, lake trout will shun the depths they may prefer later in the year and instead feed right up on top. In the spring and again in the fall, a lake's thermal stratification breaks down, and the lake trout, which normally go deep for the cooler water temperatures, may be found anywhere in the water column. It is possible at this time of year to see swirls and surface disturbances made by lakers chasing baitfish. Like the fall spawning season, this is a time of the year when a flyfisher can easily catch plenty of large lake trout.

Gaudy attractor patterns tied streamer-style in sizes 1 through 4 may be the flies you naturally reach for when you have spotted springtime lakers. These colorful attractor patterns will catch fish, but lake trout are less aggressive and more selective in the spring than in the fall. Spring fish are more interested in eating, and flies that resemble the local forage fish will draw more strikes. There are a number of streamers that can be used to imitate fleeing baitfish: the Alaska Mary Ann, the Black-Nosed Dace, the Black Ghost, the Gray Ghost, and any of the smolt patterns.

Sizes can vary according to your taste, but it doesn't make a lot of sense to use anything smaller than a size 4 or 6. Lake trout of 10 pounds, and possibly quite larger, will be cruising the topmost layer of the lake, and they have the ability to eat fairly large fish. A size 2 hook with a 3x- to 6x-long shank is a good size to use if you don't want to fool around with a lot of sizes.

Don't worry about tying a fly that is too big. One of my favorite lake trout streamers is a Gray Ghost tied on a 3/0, 6x-long shank hook. Somehow these monster hooks found their way into my collection of fly tying materials. Someone must have given them to me because I know that I didn't buy them. The only thing that I can discern on the worn label, other than the size, is that they are hand-tempered Gaelic Supremes. I had originally used them to tie a few streamers for display purposes, but a couple of flies didn't turn out to be display quality so they wound up in my streamer wallet. Later they wound up in the mouth of a lake trout, and now I tie up a few every winter to have on hand for spring lakers.

Lake Trout in Summer

Lake trout can be caught throughout the Alaskan summer. The flyfisher will most commonly encounter smaller fish up to eight pounds, with lakers closer to three pounds as the most common. Once surface layers of the water warm up, most of the larger fish head for the depths that are beyond the scope of flyfishing. Some far northern lakes, such as Chandalar, Iniakuk, and Walker, as well as many lakes throughout southwest Alaska, never see a drastic warming of the water, but even in these lakes the biggest lake trout are usually caught in the spring or fall. The fish can be anywhere in the lake during the summer, but the best places to begin searching are around areas that have irregular shorelines or bottom topography. These might be rocky points, islands, cove mouths, or quick transitions from deep to shallow water.

Studies show that food preferences of some lake trout populations change with the seasons. It is further indicated that any change in their diet probably has more to do with what is available to them as opposed to what they would prefer to eat. Small fish-imitating streamers are good flies to use if grayling, whitefish, or salmon smolts are present. Leeches are always welcome fare, and Woolly Buggers tied in black, brown, and olive work well. Sculpins are found all over Alaska, and it's always good to use imitations of them. There are all kinds of sculpin patterns, from the standard Muddler Minnow to the Mottled Woolhead Sculpin, that will work at one time or another.

Not quite as cosmopolitan as the sculpin, two species of stickleback are found in Alaska, the threespine and the ninespine stickleback. Both are often found in close association with lake trout. When they are found together, sticklebacks can be a very important forage fish for lake trout. There are a few patterns that specifically imitate the stickleback, but they are stiff and not very life-like. An excellent fly to use is an olive or brown Zonker. The rabbit strip in combination with the shiny body does a very good job of imitating the naturals, which are shades of mottled green or brown with silvery bellies. Use the Zonker to imitate sticklebacks near vegetation, and fish the sculpin along the rocks or silt of the bottom.

There are several other food items lake trout utilize. Scuds and insects may be present in the same waters as lake trout and may make up a part of their diet. Lake trout stuffed with things such as midge larvae and snails have been reported, and I once encountered a couple of lakers skimming the surface for pre-emergent midges. Even though these lakers seemed to be feeding exclusively on midges, they quickly turned and struck a streamer fished on a floating line. Hundreds of the tiny insects spilled out of their mouths as I removed the fly in preparation for their release. This illustrates an important point: lake trout will almost always go for a fish-imitating fly, even if they are feeding predominantly on something else.

During the summer, lake trout can also be taken on dry flies. On several occasions while lake fishing for grayling, lake trout have intercepted my floating fly. Conversations with other Alaskan flyfishers revealed that this occurrence was not as uncommon as it first seemed. A few of them reported catching 20 or more lake trout on dry flies in one afternoon. With my curiosity piqued, I made several trips over the ensuing summers with the sole intention of finding surface-feeding lakers rather than just relying upon incidental catches. I found that it was a surprisingly easy task. Along the Denali Highway alone, I found several lakes where the lake trout were quite susceptible to dry flies during the months of July and August. Specific patterns didn't

Lake trout. Duane Marler

seem to matter too much, and I caught lakers on everything from Wulffs to Humpies to parachutes. Rarely, however, did the fish measure more than two feet in length.

Larger fish can be caught during the summer, but the conditions have to be just right. Overcast skies are needed, and even better is to have fog sitting right on the lake's surface. Even better still is to have these conditions occur during the low light after 11 at night and before five in the morning. Skip the dry flies and use a White Woolly Bugger. I'm not sure what lake trout find so appealing about an all-white Woolly Bugger, but it seems to work wherever I encounter lakers. When I'm blind casting for lake trout during the summer—and in the spring and the fall—the White Woolly Bugger has emerged as my favorite fly.

I'll never forget one foggy July morning on a lonely mountain lake. While wading the shoreline, my fishing companions and I caught and released dozens of lake trout that ranged from two to four pounds. Just as the fog was lifting one of my partners stood on a shelf composed of the remnants of the previous winter's snows and made a long cast into dark water of unknown depths. The fly sank. He pulled in a few strips of line, and I watched him hold his rod high and listened to the whine of his reel for what seemed like an inordinate amount of time. The lake trout—or at least that's what we assumed it was—managed to strip out the entire fly line along with a couple of hundred feet of backing in one non-stop run. He never saw that fish before it retreated with his White Woolly Bugger, but I believe it was significantly bigger than four pounds. My friend became a believer in the White Woolly Bugger.

Equipment for Lake Trout

No specialized gear is needed to flyfish for lake trout. A five-weight outfit may work fine while casting dries to smaller fish, but something closer to an eight-weight is more appropriate for throwing big streamers at spring and fall fish. The main consideration, other than the size of the fish, when selecting an outfit is the size of the fly. Most fly-fishers will not feel comfortable throwing a size 2 streamer on a five- or six-weight rod. So keep the fly size in mind when selecting a rod for lake trout.

Reels should hold about 100 yards of backing, even though most average-sized lake trout will probably not use more than 50 or 60 yards. Standard leaders of seven or nine feet on floating lines and four-footers on sinking or sink-tip lines are all that is needed. Tippet strength is a personal choice, but anything over 10 pounds is usually not required. Lake trout will fight long and hard, but normally the battle takes place in open water with little opportunity to damage the leader.

Among all the species of game fish in Alaska, the lake trout has the most distinctive fighting style. When hooked, they will typically take off on a short run, pause for a moment, and then sound. Three-pound fish are very capable of bringing up the backing, and when they do, your line will be stretching down instead of out. Even if hooked in shallow water, lake trout will rarely jump. Other fish perform aerial leaps, twists, and turns. The lake trout gives the same performance but does it underwater. In clear water where this can be observed, you will often see their belly as much as their back while they are going through these underwater gyrations. It's a very different type of fight, one that must be experienced to be appreciated.

ILIAMNA PINKIE

Chapter 12
Arctic Grayling

Its large dorsal fin flared, the grayling thrashed just below the surface of the water. With my forceps, I removed the bright orange egg pattern from its mouth. The grayling held for a moment in the pocket water behind my waders. I knelt in the clear stream water, admiring the beauty, grace, and the sometimes subtle, sometimes vivid, pastel coloring which contributes to the grayling's aristocratic character. It tilted right, then left, finally regaining its equilibrium, and swam across the current into the deepest part of the pool.

On my eight-weight rod the two-pound grayling had been a mere nuisance. My main interest had been a bright school of salmon that were holding in the middle of the pool. The grayling had little chance to display its fighting capabilities against my salmon outfit, but at least I had treated it carefully and had taken a moment to observe its beautiful and graceful physical qualities. Many flyfishers will not even do that.

Usually the grayling only begins to be appreciated after a flyfisher has already conquered many other members of the salmonid family. Much of this probably has to do with its size and where it's found. A big grayling may weigh three pounds, and it may share its home water with char and trout of 10 pounds, lake trout of 30 pounds, or salmon over 50 pounds. From this standpoint, it is very easy to see which fish are going to get top billing.

The Arctic grayling (*Thymallus arcticus*) is a member of the salmonidae family and, more specifically, the sub-family thymallinae. It has a small mouth, relatively speaking, with numerous fine teeth on both jaws. Its most obvious physical characteristic is the enlarged dorsal fin, which at first viewing, seems to be much too large and irregularly shaped to belong on the grayling's elongate, cigar-shaped body. Both males and females possess this striking dorsal fin, which sometimes trails all the way back to the adipose fin. Between the rays of this dorsal fin are an assortment of dots and dashes ranging from pink to blue, while the top of the fin is finished off with a band of pink edging.

The body pattern of well-defined, large scales takes on shades of pastel colors ranging from bluish-gray to brownish-yellow. A sprinkling of black vermiculations haloed in soft blue sparsely punctuate its sides from behind the gill covers

Arctic grayling.

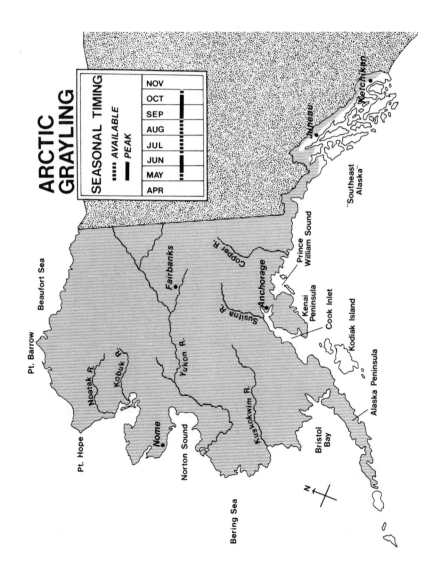

ARCTIC GRAYLING

SEASONAL TIMING

- ▪▪▪▪ AVAILABLE
- ▬ PEAK

	NOV	OCT	SEP	AUG	JUL	JUN	MAY	APR

Beaufort Sea

Pt. Barrow

Noatak R.

Kobuk R.

Fairbanks

Yukon R.

Nome

Pt. Hope

Norton Sound

Kuskokwim R.

Susitna R.

Copper R.

Anchorage

Prince William Sound

Kenai Peninsula

Cook Inlet

Kodiak Island

Alaska Peninsula

Bristol Bay

Bering Sea

Juneau

Ketchikan

"Southeast Alaska"

N

to a point somewhere between the front and the back of the dorsal fin's base.

Perhaps the most beautiful of fins on the grayling is not the dorsal at all, but instead, the pelvic fins. It's easy to ignore the smaller pelvic fins at first glance. They retain the same pastel shades as the body, but they tend to be a bit darker. This is somewhat illusionary because they may be bounded with a thin white edging. Inside the white frame, streaks of color ranging from pink to vermilion run down the fin in the same manner that paint drips from the canvas onto the edge of an easel. As striking as some of these individual parts may be, it is not any of them singly, but all of the parts of the whole that give the grayling its graceful beauty.

Undoubtedly, very few flyfishers travel to Alaska with grayling as their primary target. Instead, most visiting fly-fishers are after bigger, tackle-straining fish. But resident fly-fishers and visitors who have had the opportunity to catch grayling on light tackle quickly learn one thing—the grayling is a flyfisher's fish. Seldom dour, they can almost always be counted on to rise to a properly presented dry fly, and when they are found, it's usually in very good numbers.

Grayling: Where and When

If you did plan a trip with grayling in mind, you would want to rule out southeast Alaska and the Kenai Peninsula. Although these areas have had grayling introduced to them, and in some specific locales they may even be quite numerous, larger grayling are not common. As their name suggests, Arctic grayling are native, and most at home, throughout the interior and Arctic Alaska. Indeed, it is probably more difficult to find interior waters that do not contain grayling than those that do.

Southwest Alaska also has its share of grayling. Most of the famous rainbow trout waters of the Bristol Bay watershed also contain grayling. This is the land of trophy-sized grayling, and three-pounders are caught every year. In fact, the Alaskan record, a four-pound, thirteen-ounce grayling came from the Ugashik drainage in this area.

Seasonal timing is not as crucial a factor with grayling as it is with salmon, but there are still preferred times of the

Grayling fishing in interior Alaska.

year for the best fishing. Just after break-up in the spring, grayling crowd tributary streams in anticipation of spawning. A fish every cast is not uncommon at this time of year. Late in the fall, after they have spent an entire summer feeding on salmon eggs, the grayling may have put on an appreciable amount of weight, and many flyfishers prefer to fish for them then. Unlike so many other Alaskan fish, grayling do not show dramatic seasonal ups and downs, and excellent fishing opportunities for them can occur anytime from spring through fall.

The Life Cycle of Grayling

Grayling typically overwinter in deep sections of large rivers or in lakes and then migrate to spawning areas in the spring. The female grayling lays anywhere from 3,000 to 9,000 eggs, with the exact amount varying with the size of the fish and the stock or strain from which the fish originated. The time it takes for the eggs to hatch is heavily dependent upon the water temperature, and it can take anywhere from 11 to 30 days. Once they have emerged from the gravel, the yolk-sac-bearing young, which total about three-eighths of an inch in length, are very vulnerable to predation.

After the yolk sac disappears, the appearance of the young changes drastically, and their eyes seem disproportionately large on their almost translucent bodies. At this stage in their life, they have aptly been referred to as "two eyeballs on a string." They begin to move about quite a bit, but generally they stay near the area where they emerged. As they fill out, the dorsal fin becomes more prominent, and they may take on a black-spotted green color dorsally, with either very faint or very bold parr marks, depending upon their locality.

The grayling experience an increasing yearly growth rate until they reach the age of five. From age five until their tenth year, if they are lucky enough to reach that age, they experience a decline in growth rate. Beyond the age of 10 years, very little growth will occur, if any.

At the age of five, a grayling may range in size from eight to 15 inches. They may mature as early as two years old, but most mature at four or five years of age. In many arctic areas of Alaska, the youngest of the mature fish are age five, while others may not mature until they are eight years old. Males and females apparently mature at the same age, but in at least one study it was found that all the males had matured by age six while the females took an extra year to mature. Considering their brief life span and the fact that they usually strike flies very willingly, it is important to practice catch-and-release when fishing for grayling.

Old myths about grayling die hard, partly because there may be some truth to them and partly because there aren't too many flyfishers who concentrate on grayling fishing. If there were, the notion that a size 18 Black Gnat is a cure-all for grayling might quickly go out of fashion. Furthermore, contrary to what many people believe, catching large grayling is not always as easy as it may seem.

Just after ice-out in the spring, grayling will be concentrated for the purposes of spawning. At this time, size 8 and size 10 streamers, especially those that imitate salmon smolt or parr, can account for a banner day. Even though there may not be any emerging insects, a size 12 to 18 dry fly, such as a Humpy or an Elk Hair Caddis, may be an excellent midday producer, but subsurface flies will probably take the larger fish. This situation can occur anytime from mid-May until late June depending upon how far north you are and what the spring weather has been like.

Late June through early August present the angler with lots of daylight hours to fish for grayling, and at this time of year no flyfisher would want to be without an assortment of dry flies. Historically, the dry flies used for grayling have been the Black Gnat and the Mosquito. Both gained much of their popularity because flyfishers without any entomological background were at least aware of the presence of these biting insects in Alaska.

The mosquito doesn't imitate its namesake very well in form or function. The color isn't a very close match, and I doubt many mosquitoes can be seen floating on the surface with upright wings. But it is a buggy-looking pattern, and it fools many grayling. The Black Gnat isn't much of a realistic imitation either. To more closely imitate the black biting insect, known locally as a White Sox, a fly would have to be tied on about a size 22 hook. Throughout Alaska, Black Gnats are rarely used in a size smaller than a size 18. But the larger sizes work very well, probably due to their black silhouette, which can be easily spotted against the slate gray sky commonly seen in Alaska.

Fly Patterns for Grayling

Any flyfisher, from the East Coast to the West Coast, should be able to use his current assortment of dry flies effectively for grayling. Grayling are usually not too selective where the pattern is concerned, but they may show a preference for a particular size. Often switching from a size 12 to a size 16 will bring about many more strikes.

To make selecting an assortment of dry flies easy, think in terms of overall color and size. Pick a light, a neutral, and a dark pattern—for instance, a Light Cahill, an Adams, and a Black Gnat. Do the same with a down-wing pattern such as an Elk Hair Caddis. Then stock them in sizes from 10 to 20, and you'll have a very effective set of grayling dry flies.

For fast or broken water, you will also want to include more durable floating flies, such as a Humpy or something

Arctic grayling.

along the lines of an Irresistible. Be aware that in flat-water situations, especially in lakes, grayling will often balk at the larger, bushier flies. Keep flies simple, keep them sparse, and fish the water thoroughly.

Many of the events in Alaskan water systems revolve around the presence or absence of salmon, and even the grayling flyfisher should take note of them. In salmon-filled waters, grayling will often feed selectively on salmon roe, and at these times, a flyfisher would be lost without an appropriate fly to match it. The chenille-bodied Iliamna Pinkie and variously colored Glo-Bugs are very effective, as is any pattern that employs an egg color in its construction, such as the orange-bodied Polar Shrimp or an Orange Woolly Bugger. The Ugashik area in southwest Alaska is a prime example of this egg-feeding activity. During the month of August, grayling fattened from gorging on salmon eggs frequently top the three-pound mark.

The period just before winter's ice closes in is considered to be another prime time to catch large grayling. Surface activity might be prevalent during the warmer parts of the day, but the days will be growing short, and the chill of the morning and evening tends to dampen any aerial insect activity. Run-off water from snow-packed mountains will begin to dwindle because of the cooler temperatures, and stream conditions are likely to be low and clear. After feeding all summer long, grayling will be in the best condition of the year, and the nymph and the wet-fly fisher will be in heaven. At this time of the year, grayling will readily strike any well-presented nymph or wet fly, and of course a salmon egg imitation.

Dead-drift techniques will produce the most fish, and as with dry flies, the size, not the particular pattern, is often the most important criterion. Don't be afraid to try some of the big stuff. Some of the largest grayling I've seen fell late in the season to a slowly manipulated size 2 or 4 sculpin pattern or Woolly Bugger.

Tactics for Grayling

If you have fished for trout and are familiar with the importance of and the numerous ways of presenting a drag-free fly, you will have no problem catching grayling. Grayling are often much more forgiving than trout, and they will often take a fly even after it has begun to drag. In fact, there are some occasions when grayling will show a preference for a dry fly that is skittered across the current. Once a fly begins to swing around and pick up speed at the end of a drift, a grayling will sometimes chase the fly, possibly missing it three or four times before sharpening its aim and getting hooked. This commonly occurs in shallow riffles at the tailout of a pool.

One reason that grayling are prone to missing dry flies is due to the manner in which they sometimes strike them. Rather than sucking in the fly from below, grayling will often leap clear of the water and take the fly on the way back down. They don't do it all the time, and I don't have a clue as to why they do it other than that they're simply showing off. When you see it I think you'll agree that it's one of the strangest— and most graceful—strikes in the world of dry-fly fishing.

There are times when grayling will sulk in the deeper parts of a stream. Holding in what seem to be very advantageous feeding lanes, they may refuse several offerings, and after some observation it may seem as though they are not even feeding on the naturals. The key for success here is to keep a low profile and keep casting to them. Change flies and show them new stuff, repeatedly. Once one of the smaller fish from the pool, and it will almost always be a small one, decides to take a fly, the barrier will be broken. Release it quickly because the next cast or two will invariably bring another strike. It seems that sometimes a school of grayling need the impetus of a feeding fish to get the rest of them in the mood to strike. Once one individual does make that initial attack, it spurs on the rest of them to begin feeding. It's a rather odd behavioral characteristic, but it has even been mentioned in the scientific literature.

Another notable characteristic flyfishers should be aware of is the manner in which grayling frequently position themselves in a pool. In almost all cases, the largest fish will be closest to the head of the pool. Usually two or three of the largest fish will hold at the head of the pool, just below the point where the main current enters. From here to some midway point in the pool, depending upon how large the pool is and how many fish are occupying it, the size of the fish will get progressively smaller. Once a point is reached where many of the fish are relatively the same size, the hierarchy tends to break down, and the fish continually change positions.

Because of this hierarchy, it is an obvious advantage to attempt to drift the fly through the uppermost section of a pool where grayling are suspected of holding. Sometimes it may require beginning the drift in the riffle above the pool so that the artificial enters as naturally as possible. Without this intent in mind, your fly may not have sunk to the correct depth or may be floating outside the main feeding lane when it passes the largest fish. Only when it had passed the mid-point of the pool would it be effectively presented.

Flyfishing for grayling in lakes can range from being ridiculously simple to extremely challenging. There are times when they will strike any dry fly, wet fly, nymph, or streamer that hits the water. The trouble arises when they are zeroing in on only dry flies. Often they will hit almost any dry fly, but at other times they will be much more selective, taking only one size or color.

Sometimes, when grayling are rising all around me for emerging midges, I get no response with dry flies, even when I use a fly that imitates the natural very closely. I

Releasing a grayling.

make long casts and short casts. I work my way all the way down to 7x tippets. I try nymphs, emergers, and several styles of dry flies. I try numerous retrieves, and I also try letting the fly just sit there for a long time. Nothing works.

Each winter when I am analyzing my fishing journal, I spend an inordinate amount of time on the entries that describe these occurrences. I still haven't figured out any new tactics to try. In a way, I think it's kind of refreshing to be humbled by one of Alaska's smallest fish.

Equipment for Grayling

Since grayling are relatively small fish, it stands to reason that the new generation of light rods, matched with three-, two- or even one-weight lines, would complement them nicely. In fact, they do. It's a delight to throw small dries and wets with these seven- to nine-foot lightweight rods to actively feeding grayling under beautiful weather conditions.

But there are three major drawbacks to using gear that is this light. First, weather conditions are usually not too conducive to using these light sticks. In many areas of Alaska, especially on the open tundra, the wind can blow enough to rule out using them. Secondly, they just aren't built to handle and do not perform well with the big, heavily-weighted flies that are sometimes needed to catch large grayling. And lastly, mammoth-sized rainbow trout and char may also inhabit the same waters as grayling, and a two-weight outfit may not be what you prefer to use if you hook into the rainbow of a lifetime.

A more sensible all-around outfit for grayling fishing in Alaska would be a four-, five-, or six-weight. An average rod length of nine feet is fine, but there are lots of opinions about rod length, so let your personal preference dictate the length. I have used many outfits for grayling, but the majority of the time I will settle on an eight-and-a-half foot, four-weight rod or a nine-foot, five-weight rod.

When fishing for grayling, as with most trout fishing, the reel does not do much more than store the line. Select a reel that balances well with the rod you have chosen. Backing is usually not a major consideration, but keep in mind that an unseen trout or char of three or four times the proportions of the largest grayling may intercept your fly at any time. With this in mind, and to keep your fly line from being coiled too tightly, it is always a good idea to fill your reel with its maximum backing capacity.

As when fishing for any other species of fish in Alaska, you will be met with extreme variations of weather and water conditions. The best way to meet these conditions is with an assortment of lines. A floating line is essential for grayling, because depending upon what time of year it is, they just may be the only fish that you will get to rise to a dry fly. Fishing a dry fly can be a pleasant reprieve after you have spent a couple of days fishing fast-sinking lines with heavily-weighted flies in pursuit of salmon.

More often than not, however, you will need to present your fly at some depth below the surface. This is especially true when fishing smolt patterns and egg imitations. Depending upon your preference, you can use a sink-tip line, a floating line with split shot attached to the leader, a weighted fly, or a combination of these methods. Although grayling will move upward in the water column much more so than most Alaskan fish, your primary goal when fishing subsurface patterns is still to present your fly at the level of the fish. Your decisions on what methods to employ should be guided by the speed of the current and how deep the fish are holding. If you carry lines with various sink rates, most of the time you will be able to skip the split shot and retain a pleasant casting rhythm.

Grayling are rarely leader shy. A seven-foot leader with a four-pound tippet is a good choice when fishing dry flies or when presenting wets or nymphs just below the surface. Of course with a sink-tip line, you'll want short leaders—four feet is about right. If you choose to use a floating line with split shot attached to the leader, leaders up to 12 feet long may be appropriate.

From southwest Alaska through upper Cook Inlet and all the way up onto the North Slope, grayling are never too far away. A flyfisher with appropriately light tackle can expect to enjoy catching grayling at any time of year from ice-out until freeze-up. Almost any flyfisher will be able to hook and release many small fish in the course of one day. But be observant, because it is the flyfisher who takes the time to assess the situation and use the most appropriate techniques who will have the best chance of consistently catching the largest Arctic grayling from any stream or lake.

DAHLBERG DIVER

Chapter 13
Northern Pike

I vividly recall one evening of fishing in a small cove of a lake in the Bristol Bay region. I had spotted lots of emergent vegetation in the cove on my way to do some char fishing, and I made a point to return there a couple of hours before sunset. When I returned, I cut the outboard engine well outside of the cove and used the oars to bring the boat into the shallows. Pike can be skittish when they are in the shallows, and even without the engine running I managed to scare some fish. The only evidence of their departure was swirls on the water's surface.

When I finally stood up to take a look, I became very excited. Long, dark forms of pike were all over the cove. Just within my field of view there must have been 25 or 30 pike.

Without thinking, I knotted a red and white Maraflash Fly to the 2x tippet I had been using. The first cast resulted in a swirl, a strike, and a very short fight as the little northern quickly sliced right through my leader. I didn't have any shock tippets with me, but I managed to fashion a leader out

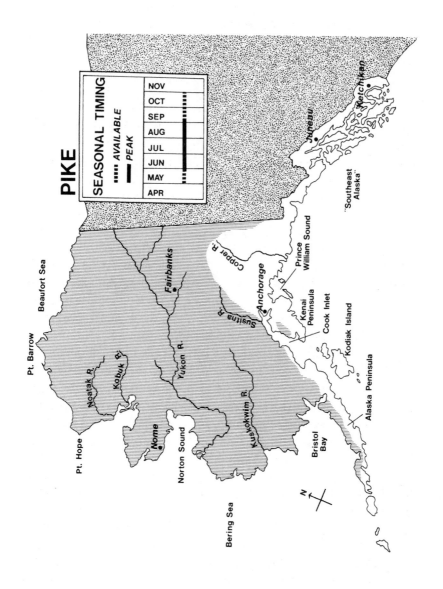

PIKE

SEASONAL TIMING

..... AVAILABLE
▬▬ PEAK

NOV	
OCT	
SEP	
AUG	
JUL	
JUN	
MAY	
APR	

of the butt sections of several lighter leaders. I now had 30-pound test at the terminal end of my leader, and to this I attached a size 2 Spruce Streamer. The next cast brought the same results—a quick hit and a sliced line.

I became frantic. Muttering to myself something about being unprepared, I scattered the contents of my gear bag on the bottom of the boat. The search turned up a single piece of wire about 15 inches long. In a hurry, I managed to screw up the Albright knot twice before I finally got it right. Now I was down to 12 inches of wire, but it worked. For the next two hours I caught and released over two dozen pike. Not one in the lot was over five pounds, so had I kept fishing with a monofilament tippet, I'm sure that I would have eventually landed a fish. But Alaska's pike are not leader shy, so why take a chance with mono when you can have the insurance of wire? Even if you're catching relatively small pike, you never know when that 15- or 20-pounder is going to appear following your fly.

Northern pike (*Esox lucius*) are brownish-olive dorsally with irregular rows of markings along their sides. Their bellies are an unmarked creamy-white to yellowish color. They have a broad, flat snout suggestive of a duck's bill, and their overall body shape is long and slender.

Pike: Where and When

Northern pike are found throughout Alaska's lakes and rivers. Pike are fairly abundant everywhere, except for the Southeast and parts of south-central Alaska. However, there is at least one isolated population in the Southeast, and they have also been introduced (not under the auspices of any agency) to areas on the Kenai Peninsula and the Susitna River drainage. Most of these fish are the two- or three-pound variety known as hammer handles, so anyone with specific intentions of presenting a fly to a pike should head north.

The Minto Flats area near Fairbanks is a major hot spot for pike. By being relatively close to a major population center, Fairbanks, and by having fairly easy access via riverboat or floatplane, Minto Flats has developed an excellent reputation for pike fishing. However, there are literally thousands of other lakes and sloughs throughout interior Alaska,

Arctic Alaska, and down into southwest Alaska where pike can be found.

Pike can be caught by the flyfisher in Alaska throughout the spring, summer, and fall seasons. Pike may migrate, but often it is nothing more than a local movement to and from shallow-water spawning areas. Typically, the largest pike are most available to flyfishers in the spring, after which time they normally move off to deeper waters.

Pike are spring spawners, and immediately after ice-out, they can be found spawning in the shallow areas of lakes. The eggs hatch in one to four weeks, and the young feed opportunistically on many different organisms. Growth during the first year is rapid, and as soon as they have reached a sufficient size, they begin to feed on other fish. Once pike have switched to this fish diet, they are just as likely to eat their siblings as any other fish that swims past.

Fly Patterns for Pike

It is often said that the northern pike of Alaska will hit anything that you throw at them. To some degree this is true. If you're fishing a shallow inlet during midsummer for two- to four-pound fish, there is a good chance that they will hit any fly that you cast to them. But to catch larger pike with any regularity, your choice of fly will be more important.

In the spring, big pike will be in the shallows, and they'll be aggressive. This is the time to get the larger fish on floating flies. There are a variety of mouse, shrew, and lemming flies, and they will all work at this time of year. Keep the pattern simple. It doesn't take very many pike to completely destroy a fly, so don't bother using a pattern that is expensive or one that takes a long time to tie. A simple oblong, clipped deer-hair mouse will work fine. There is also another advantage to a simple pattern. When you add eyes, whiskers, legs, and a tail it just makes the fly heavier, and it is already tough enough to cast something that resembles a floating spruce cone.

Throughout the rest of the year, it will not be as easy to get large pike to come to the fly. Just like any other fish, large pike become accustomed to a particular food source, and the flyfisher who uses a fly that imitates the local forage fish will be the most successful. Any young salmon that may be pres-

Northern pike.

ent are fair game, but large pike may prefer an even bigger meal. Grayling and whitefish make a much more substantial meal for big fish. This doesn't mean that you have to search through the flyfishing literature for flies that imitate grayling and whitefish, because there already are some patterns that will do nicely. Two flies that immediately come to mind are the Gray Ghost and the Alaska Mary Ann. Both have coloration that is similar to whitefish and grayling, and the silver pheasant body feathers used for the shoulders of the Gray Ghost provide a nice fish-like silhouette.

Pike are generally very aggressive fish, so you should never rule out attractor patterns. The Flash Fly, so popular with Alaskan silver salmon flyfishers, can be deadly when stripped fast through deep water for pike. Bucktails of various colors, especially two-color patterns such as red and white, blue and white, and green and white, have resulted in many good days of pike fishing. And the Mickey Finn with its good old red-and-yellow combination is a pattern that I wouldn't want to be without on pike waters.

Pike have the ability to spit out flies quickly after they have inhaled them. Slim or sparsely-tied flies can be rapidly expelled, and it is for this reason that I prefer flies for pike that are very fully tied. Large, fluffy patterns that have lots of marabou or saddle hackle are much tougher for a pike to spit out. Alaskabous are particularly effective in delaying a pike's expulsion of the fly.

The traveling angler who fishes for the big fish of southern saltwater will already have an excellent pike fly selection. Tarpon flies and Lefty's Deceivers are great flies for pike. The McNally Magnum and the Dahlberg Diver also represent nice large entrees for pike.

Although they're not used too often, tube flies work very well for pike. Tied on lightweight plastic tubing, the result is a fly that is very large but relatively light for its size. Since the hook is not attached to the fly, it is easy to switch to the size appropriate for the situation.

Rabbit-strip flies are, however, quickly displacing all others as the most popular type of fly to use for pike. Colorfully-dyed rabbit strips can be wrapped around the hook shank, left trailing beyond the bend of the hook or both. The colors selected can imitate the venerable red-and-yellow Mickey

Pike in backwater slough.

Finn—or any other pattern—and offer a enticing, pulsating action in the water that is equally as attractive to the fish as marabou is. Rabbit-strip flies can be more quickly constructed than many traditional patterns and are much more durable than other undulating materials, such as marabou, and the pike love them. Consequently, they are the choice of many professional guides.

The question of what size fly to use is always a concern, and with pike, bigger is better. It is not uncommon for a pike to take a meal that is almost 20 percent of its own body size. So when you are looking for pike in the 15-pound category, it would be difficult to use a fly that is too large. My personal assortment of pike flies has creations that are tied on hooks as large as 4/0, but generally anything size 4 or larger is fine.

Tactics for Pike

It's important to be aware of the differences between northern pike and most other Alaskan game fish. Unlike many of the salmonids, pike will not be found in the fast water of rivers. They just aren't built for it.

Instead, their streamlined bodies are designed for acceleration, allowing them to overtake their prey, even fast-moving prey. As a result, some type of retrieve is almost always necessary to attract their attention, and only in rare instances will they take a fly that is dead-drifted.

Casting to open water, unless the fish are very deep, is usually a waste of time. Debris, stumps, undercut banks, or downed trees are good places to prospect for pike, but the most typical pike haunts are in and around aquatic vegetation. Around lily pads, emergent grasses, or a combination of the two are undoubtedly the most productive areas to present a fly to pike.

In Alaska these prime locations for pike can be found in both rivers and lakes, but in rivers look particularly for backwaters and slow-moving side channels with vegetation. Cast close to likely-looking spots and use a variety of different retrieves. Fast, short strips will often elicit the predatory instincts in pike. At other times, they may prefer to stalk the fly over a long distance before engulfing it. Often, when they are in this mood, they'll take the fly as it stops between

Flyfishing for pike.

two slow, foot-long pulls. Here you will have to pay very close attention, because the strike is almost undetectable.

Equipment for Pike

If you are gearing up specifically for pike, start with a stout rod that handles an eight-weight line. The rod should have a lot of backbone for two reasons: you will be throwing large, wind-resistant flies, and you will need lifting power if you are fishing from a boat. You will not get long, sizzling runs or acrobatic leaps from these fish, but the big ones will put a full bend in your rod and keep it there for quite a while. Once the fight nears a close, pulling the fish toward you requires a beefy rod. It is no easy trick to pull 15 pounds of pike through the water, even if it has ceased to struggle violently.

In the spring, floating lines can be used for large pike, but during the heat of summer the big ones often head for deeper water. In these situations, sink-tip and full-sinking lines will be needed. Alaskan weather and water conditions typically vary from day to day, and it makes good sense to have a full selection of lines.

There isn't any need to duplicate your gear, and your eight-weight salmon outfit can easily be put into service for pike. The reel isn't crucial. One with a palm-controlled drag and 100 yards of backing is more than adequate. The only adjustment you will need to make is to your leader. A 12-

inch section of wire for a tippet, attached to the monofilament with an Albright knot, will do nicely.

I find that braided wire coated with plastic is the easiest kind to use. It is conveniently carried on a spool, it doesn't kink readily, and as far as wire goes, it is not too difficult to tie knots with. A figure-eight or a Homer Rhode loop knot can be used to attach the fly to the wire. Regardless of the differences in knot strength, the Homer Rhode loop knot has a definite advantage over the figure-eight knot. The open loop of the Homer Rhode knot allows the fly to swing freely and more enticingly when it is being retrieved.

To say that pike have sharp teeth is truly an understatement. Even wire leaders may eventually fray and break after several fish. As you attempt to get your fly back from a pike brought to your side, you will immediately become familiar with the pike's arsenal of teeth. Just one quick look at its gaping maw will confirm why hemostats or long-nosed pliers are an absolute must when removing your fly. Once you have the fish in a position to be released, be extremely careful. I once had the opportunity to observe what a carelessly handled two-pound pike can do to a thumb and forefinger— luckily they weren't my own.

The safest way to grasp small to moderate-sized pike is over the top of the head while applying light pressure to the gill plates with your fingers. Very large specimens will probably have to be netted and worked on by two people. While one person uses two hands to restrain the fish, a second person can remove the fly. Under no circumstances should you ever hold the fish by inserting your fingertips into its eye sockets. This barbaric, but often used, practice is wrong. Never do it to any fish that is going to be released.

Very few flyfishers will ever venture all the way into Alaska's bush with the sole intention of catching pike, but they are a worthy game fish. Found throughout a large part of Alaska, pike waters are often not far from the environs of more sought-after fish. After having many enjoyable outings for pike, I would encourage any flyfisher to take some time out and try for them. Who knows, even though you may have some negative, preconceived notions, you may find that you like pike.

BUMBLE PUPPY

Chapter 14
Sheefish

I had read a little bit about them. Very little that is, because sheefish don't show up too frequently in print. But here I was in mid-August casting a white Lefty's Deceiver into the waters of the Hoholitna River. I'd been casting for quite a while, and because sheefish are often referred to as "tarpon of the north," my thoughts had drifted to tarpon fishing. I was thinking of big tarpon, the ones over 100 pounds that I'd never landed. Just then, I felt some resistance at the end of my line, and reacting in the tarpon mode, I pointed my rod straight toward the fish and pulled the line back as hard as I could with my left hand. Whatever had mouthed my fly must have been surprised, as I quickly and efficiently popped the eight-pound tippet.

After tying on another Lefty's Deceiver, I fished for the next half hour without a bump. In the mood for a change, I tied on a size 2 Flash Fly, and within a couple of casts I was rewarded with another tug on my line. This time I didn't react quite as severely as I had on the first strike, and as I put a bend in the rod, a five-pound sheefish catapulted itself out of the water. The small sheefish didn't take too much line, but it fought gamely and made three or four more jumps before I got it in close enough to get a good look.

With the sheefish still thrashing, the hook popped out just as I got my forceps on it. It had some fight left, and it made two half-hearted leaps as it moved back into the river current. That small sheefish and the several others that I landed before the afternoon was over brought back memories. Memories not of Alaska, but of warmer places with mangroves and always eager-to-jump baby tarpon. It was easy to see how the sheefish in Alaska had earned the nickname "tarpon of the tundra."

Also called inconnu by the French voyagers (which translates to "unknown"), sheefish (*Stenodus leucichthys*) are unique among the sport fish Alaska has to offer. They belong to the whitefish family, but they are distinguished from other members of the family by their large mouth and their protruding lower jaw. Their overall body color is silver with a bluish to purple tint. Their body shape is considered elongate, and even the largest individuals retain a streamlined profile. At first glance the large cycloid scales seem too large in relation to the body size. This is especially true when the fish are removed from the water on a bright day, allowing the sun's reflections to trick the eye.

Male and female fish of the species are similar in appearance, but normally the females live to older ages and, as a result, the largest fish are usually females. Sheefish of 10 to 15 pounds are common in some areas, and a record 53-pounder was taken from the Kobuk River drainage in August of 1986. There are also scattered reports of much larger sheefish having been observed in the same watershed.

Sheefish: Where and When

In Alaska the sheefish is found in several areas of the Arctic and the interior. The Kuskokwim, Yukon, and the Selawik-Kobuk river drainages are their principal home waters. The only other populations of sheefish are found in parts of northern Canada and in Siberia.

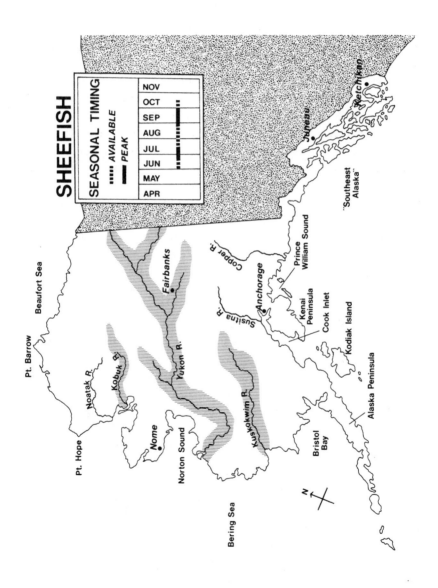

SHEEFISH

SEASONAL TIMING

···· AVAILABLE
▬ PEAK

NOV	
OCT	
SEP	
AUG	
JUL	
JUN	
MAY	
APR	

Fisheries biologists further differentiate sheefish by acknowledging distinct populations in specific geographic areas of Alaska: the Kuskokwim River, the lower Yukon River, the middle Yukon River, the upper Yukon River, the Koyukuk River, and the Selawik and Kobuk rivers. Even within these areas, they have identified additional independent populations, bringing the total to nine distinct populations of sheefish. They have also concluded that among these nine groups, five are local freshwater populations, and four are estuarine-anadromous. These latter groups roughly follow a typical anadromous life cycle in that they spawn in freshwater and then spend part of their lives in saltwater. They do not, however, roam the ocean as a salmon does, but instead remain in brackish lakes or in estuaries.

Over the past 15 years only a limited amount of scientific investigation has been directed toward the sheefish. What little has been done is very informative for the angler, but there are still many gaps. Without the wealth of literature that surrounds other sport fish, there are many places yet to be publicized that offer excellent opportunities for the fly-fisher to take sheefish.

The Kobuk River is by far the most talked about destination for sheefish anglers. Although many of them discuss it, very few actually make it there. There are at least a couple of guides that operate on the Kobuk, and they bring in a fair number of clients. However, if you venture to the Kobuk River, you won't have to worry about crowds. The Kobuk drainage and most other places where sheefish are found are largely wilderness areas that see relatively few visiting anglers or tourists.

Sheefish action begins in the lower reaches of the Kobuk River right after the ice has melted. Lots of fish are available at this time, but the river is usually very high with run-off water and almost all of the fishing has to be done from a boat. The movement of the fish in June from their brackish-water wintering grounds is the result of two factors. They are following schools of forage fish, in this case it's the least cisco (*Coregonus sardinella*), and they are also beginning their upstream migration.

By July and into August, the sheefish will arrive in the middle reaches of the Kobuk River. Still feeding voraciously, they are now a much easier target for the flyfisher. In late August and September, the sheefish will be even further upstream, and it is then that conditions are excellent for fly-fishing. Prevailing low water conditions expose large beaches and gravel bars, giving the flyfisher a great shot at passing or holding fish.

There's no doubt that the Kobuk River in mid-September is my number one choice for a time and a place to pursue shee-fish. Besides having good fishing for sheefish, the Kobuk River above the Arctic Circle can be a gloriously wonderful place. Yes, the wind can blow and it can rain and snow, but seeing the golden and red colors of the tundra and herds of migrating caribou on the few bluebird days that you do get make it all worth it.

Some people claim that the fight of an early-season shee-fish is far more exciting than that of a late-season fish. This is a highly plausible but subjective claim, yet I have never heard of anyone complaining about the fight of a fall sheefish.

The Kobuk River does have the largest sheefish in Alaska. This is backed up by both angling reports and research liter-ature. But it does not hold the greatest number of sheefish. It is the Yukon River that contains the greatest population of sheefish. The Yukon River, though, is a large and silty river, and the main body of water does not hold too much promise for the flyfisher. A flyfisher's best bet is to be there in the month of July and to explore tributary streams that enter its lower reaches. Other good prospects for catching sheefish on the fly are the Koyukuk, the Melozitna, and the Holitna rivers.

The Life Cycle of the Sheefish

Sheefish are fall spawners, and in most places spawning takes place sometime between late September and mid-October. The anadromous fish that spend their winter in large river estuaries begin the migration to their spawning grounds immediately after break-up. Depending on the par-ticular group of fish, this migration may last anywhere from two weeks to four months. Along this journey, the sheefish may linger in one area to feed for a while, but once they're on their spawning grounds they refrain from feeding.

Releasing a sheefish.

Sheefish typically spawn in clear-water streams in three to 10 feet of water. They don't build redds, but instead are broadcast spawners. The female, accompanied by a male who swims below her, rises toward the surface at the upstream end of the spawning area, releasing her eggs while the male ejects his milt. The eggs drift through the cloud of milt as they sink to the bottom. This pass over the spawning bed may take place several times, because larger females can contain well over 100,000 eggs. Because the eggs are released high in the water column in rather swift currents, the type of stream bottom is very important in selection of sheefish spawning sites. A substratum of irregularly-shaped gravel or rock helps catch the eggs as they sink to the bottom.

Once they've spawned, sheefish begin a fairly rapid return to their wintering areas. This may be saltwater for the anadromous groups or the deep holes of large rivers for the non-anadromous groups. Because sheefish feed during their spawning journey, they reach their spawning grounds in good physical condition, and unlike Alaska's salmon, they live to spawn again.

Cold Arctic waters cause the eggs to develop slowly, and it may be five to seven months before the young fish emerge from the gravel. The juveniles, even though they remain in cold waters, grow rapidly during their first two years of life. At two years of age, a sheefish will average eight inches in length and will have already adopted the piscivorous diet that will sustain it throughout its life. Growth rates, size attained, and age at sexual maturity vary considerably among the different groups of fish. Fish from the Kuskokwim River may reach heavier weights at eight to 10 years of age, but the largest fish are the slower-growing specimens of the Kobuk River drainage. Here a fish may reach 50 pounds or more and may be 20 to 25 years old.

Fly Patterns for Sheefish

Sheefish are the predators of the whitefish family. Although very small fish may feed on a number of invertebrates, adults are almost exclusively piscivorous. Like many fish, their food preferences depend upon the seasonal availability of forage fishes. Ciscoes and whitefish, because they are found in high densities within the home waters of sheefish, are often preferred food items. But sheefish aren't necessarily finicky eaters, and any other fish, including char, juvenile salmon, suckers, smelt, sticklebacks, and sculpins, are not exempt from their jaws.

With this latter piece of information in mind, flyfishers shouldn't have any difficulty assembling a collection of flies that will be of interest to sheefish. Baitfish patterns, many of the same ones intended for lake trout and pike, will work at any time of the season for sheefish. A large smolt pattern, a Janssen Minnow, or a Winnipesaukee Smelt are excellent flies to try when sheefish are on the prowl near the surface.

White-bodied flies often work well, and the Alaska Mary Ann, which had its beginnings in the Kobuk area, is one such fly. According to one version of the story, people in the Kotzebue area used a piece of ivory, some polar bear hair, and a bent nail as a jig, or "Kobuk hook" as they called it, for sheefish. Then a gentleman named Frank Dufresne began to use these Kobuk hooks on his fly rod and eventually imitated them with a fly. Supposedly the woman who gave him the Kobuk hooks was named Mary Ann, and therefore he called this new fly the Alaska Mary Ann.

Another lesser-known fly that has had good reports in conjunction with sheefish is the Bumble Puppy. One version of this fly, and there are many, calls for a white chenille body, silver tinsel rib, white bucktail wing, red hackle-fiber tail, and a teal body feather tied in as a collar. Some fly tiers also add a band of red chenille as a butt or egg sac. Its general appearance is not a lot different than that of the Alaska Mary Ann, and I suppose it just goes to show how effective a mostly-white fly can be for sheefish.

A well-rounded flyfisher will probably already have several other flies that sheefish will strike. Streamer patterns that imitate baitfish are too numerous to name, and many of them, even those that have never been cast into sheefish waters, would probably do a fine job of fooling sheefish. One notable pattern is the Abel Anchovy. Designed by reel maker Steve Abel for sharks off the California coast, it would be my choice if I only had one fly to use for sheefish.

Several different styles of flies can be adapted to imitate an escaping baitfish. Among them are the Zonkers, Matukas, Thunder Creeks, and Deceivers. Although I have not personally tried them on sheefish, the Blondes, popularized by Joe Brooks for saltwater fishing, look as though they may work well for sheefish.

Like most other Alaskan sport fish, sheefish are susceptible to flies other than those that imitate their preferred food. At times, attractor patterns are also taken readily. The choice of an attractor pattern rarely follows any guidelines. Most selections have as their only criterion the whim of the angler. Colorful flies like the Mickey Finn or any other bicolored or tricolored bucktails are worth trying. Flyfishers who tie their own flies often make up assortments of various-colored flies tied with Fishair instead of bucktail. The addition of a little Flashabou or similar material doesn't hurt, and it is usually added to these flies. An infinite number of color combinations are used, but the most popular colors

Kobuk River sheefish. Rich Landers.

seem to be blue, yellow, and green. Also, because sheefish often inhale a fly, large flies are not out of the question, and the many different styles of tarpon flies will take fish.

This brings us to the question of hook size and style. There isn't a best sheefish hook because tradeoffs have to be made when considering the size, type, finish, and wire strength of a hook, but here are some guidelines. Sheefish have extremely strong jaws, and they have been known to bend hooks, so look for strong, stout hooks. Sizes can range from 2 to 4/0 depending upon the style of hook selected and the type of fly you intend to tie. You will also want to have the versatility of both weighted and unweighted flies. And lastly, if you think that you may be fishing in the early part of the season, you will want to select a corrosion-resistant hook for use in brackish waters.

Although sheefish are called tarpon of the north because of their aerial acrobatics, the similarity doesn't end there. They also have very large scales, and most importantly, they possess a very bony mouth. There are spots in the mouth with soft tissues, but even so, it is very important to keep your hook points razor sharp. Check them frequently, especially when you are fishing a fly deep over a rocky bottom.

Tactics for Sheefish

To watch the spectacular fight of a sheefish, you first have to hook one, and although it's not difficult to do, here are some tactics that will increase your chances. First of all, there is no substitute for employing the services of a good guide. Sheefish are wanderers, and it's not unusual for them to be moving throughout the summer. A spot that is packed with sheefish may be barren the following week. It's very simple—either go in with a hit-or-miss attitude or hire a guide who lives on the river.

If you don't hire a guide, the next best way to find sheefish is to float the river. You should be aware, though, that they will probably not be found along the entire length of the river. Sheefish will almost always be inconsistently distributed. Some sections of river will be loaded with fish, and then, possibly for long periods of time, you'll float through dead areas. The key to success here is to search continually for fish while you are drifting. When you do find them, pull over and work the water both upstream and downstream.

Sometimes the water conditions of mid- to late season will permit you to cast to sighted fish. This is obviously an exciting way to fish, but more often than not, you will not be sight-fishing for your quarry. When you can't spot the fish, you'll have to learn to recognize the type of holding water they prefer, which is not very difficult to do.

Sheefish like to avoid the strongest river currents. So it is really very easy to find their holding lies. Any type of obstruction that creates slack water behind it is a likely spot. Midstream gravel bars or islands create that type of spot. The inside corners of bends in the river and where backwater sloughs enter and exit are prime locations. In short, sheefish are likely to hold anywhere there is some quiet water.

When sheefish are visibly feeding near the surface, quickly stripping an unweighted streamer across the top using a floating line usually results in a strike. When you're prospecting in the slower waters of a deep river, a slow retrieve is best. Approach your target area from an across-and-upstream position. Gradually lengthen your casts so that your fly drifts farther back into the slow water on each successive cast. Regardless of the fly pattern you are using, it is almost always best to strip the fly in as slowly as possible. Inch the fly in with a short strip-pause-short strip sequence.

Of course, sheefish will sometimes hit a faster-moving fly, and as in any fishing situation, it's a good idea to experiment with different retrieves, techniques, and approaches. However, the flyfisher who can consistently work the fly slow and deep will be the most successful the majority of the time.

Flyfishers who have been on the river when sheefish action has been nonstop throughout an entire day may find it hard to believe, but there are often better times of the day to try for sheefish. From first light until mid-morning is almost always a productive time. You have to keep in mind that, because of continuous daylight above the Arctic Circle in midsummer, distinctions between morning, noon, and night are often rather fuzzy. Later in the season, when a more normal day and night sequence returns, fishing at either end of the day is best.

Equipment for Sheefish

The tackle necessary for sheefish varies depending upon the time of the year and the region you are fishing. The high water of the early season sometimes necessitates fishing with sink-tips, full-sinking lines, and high-density sinking shooting tapers. However, conditions can change rapidly, and if you happen to be at the right spot when a school of baitfish passes by, you may be able to switch to a floating line. In these instances, you can cast to sheefish that are leaving wakes on the surface as they chase ciscoes and whitefish.

Outside of the Kobuk drainage, in areas where fish over 20 pounds are uncommon, an eight-weight rod is quite suitable. I prefer a long rod, something in the vicinity of nine-and-a-half feet. It may be more psychological than anything, but I feel that an extra half foot gives me a big advantage when mending line. The only problem with an eight-weight outfit may be in handling very large flies that are heavily weighted. If the fish are showing a preference for large flies and are holding in very deep water, the only option may be to go with a heavier outfit.

Short leaders, four feet and less, are the norm when fishing sinking lines. Even with a floating line, anything over seven feet long is rarely necessary because sheefish are not leader shy. Unless you're fishing an area that is full of underwater obstructions, eight-, 10-, and 12-pound tippets are sufficient.

Reels of the caliber suited to eight- to 10-weight lines will invariably hold enough backing to handle any sheefish. As with any fly reel, it is a good idea to have as much backing as its capacity will allow. Extremely long runs are not characteristic of sheefish, and rarely will you see a lot of backing go through your guides. Some flyfishers have their heavier-weight systems matched with anti-reverse reels, and while these are fine for sheefish, they aren't necessary. It is important to note, though, that early season fishing may take you into brackish water, and it is wise to use a reel that can withstand exposure to saltwater.

Sometimes it is said that the way a fish strikes the fly dictates the nature of the entire fight. Nothing could be more true with sheefish. When a sheefish decides it wants your fly, the take is in no way gentle, subtle, or slow to develop. Often the strike will be about as subtle as a swift kick to your shins. Furious water-splashing antics will follow immediately, and while the fight may last for hours, a sheefish will give every ounce of itself during every second of the fight. Aerial acrobatics are one of their trademarks, and it's not uncommon for a sheefish to get some "air time" three or four times in quick succession. Sometimes the fish refrain from actually clearing the water, but even when a sheefish is in one of these non-jumping moods, most of the fight will take place right on top.

Many well-traveled anglers have never encountered the sheefish, but this has nothing to do with the sporting qualities of the fish. They take a fly readily and they fight gamely, but the pristine settings where they are commonly found are difficult or expensive to get to—even by Alaska's standards. It takes a little bit of extra effort to make a sheefish excursion a reality, but any extra effort is well worth it to fish for this unique trophy of the north.

EVERGLOW FLY

Chapter 15
Flyfishing
Alaskan Saltwater

The saltwater of Resurrection Bay in south-central Alaska is not a common destination for flyfishers, a fact that was quite obvious from the looks we were getting from anglers in passing boats. They were trolling for silver salmon with flashers and twirling herring without any luck. We were drifting and double hauling baitfish patterns with the same results.

Even though we were not catching any fish, it was still great to be out on the water. A flat, calm July morning in Resurrection Bay is not something that you soon forget. Mountains that seemed to come right up out of the edge of the bay provided a spectacular backdrop for the setting. Sea otters floated on their backs, bald eagles cruised the shorelines looking for easy pickings, and puffins flew around and then landed with the grace of a rock hitting the water.

However, the splash that caught my attention was not caused by a bird but by a fish. I turned in time to see the splash but not the fish. Within a minute my partner snapped his rod back just after his fly had hit the water, and I heard the sound of his reel. I tensed up waiting for a strike of my own. You can't always be sure you will find salmon in saltwater, but when you find one, you can bet that it is not alone. But I didn't get a hit, and instead of casting again I sat back to watch.

I was really quite excited, but the herring twirlers had noticed our hook-up. I thought it would be much more impressive to assume an air of nonchalance as they swung in for a close pass. They came in closer than I had expected, and as we bobbed in their passing wake I distinctly heard the words, "silver" and "luck." Although I am not sure of the exact context, you can be fairly sure that they were wondering how two guys with fly rods in a skiff could be catching silver salmon when they weren't.

It was at about this time that we realized that the salmon was not a silver. Instead it was a pink. The fish was released, and our next casts resulted in a double hook-up. Evidently a group of fish had just moved into the area, and for the next couple of hours we were in pink heaven. We didn't catch any silvers, but we caught pinks on every couple of casts.

This event took place several seasons ago, and it pops into my mind every time someone asks me about flyfishing saltwater in Alaska. It is not memorable because it was my first flyfishing trip in Alaska's saltwater and not for the number of pink salmon that we caught nor for the lack of silver salmon. It remains memorable because of that first pink salmon, the pink that, for quite a while, had us thinking it was a silver salmon.

Anyone who has caught both pink and silver salmon in freshwater rivers, as we both had, would find it hard to believe that a pink salmon could fool you into thinking it was a silver salmon. Silvers are renowned and respected for their fighting ability, while pinks are not usually held in high regard. Silvers hold up well in freshwater but pinks deteriorate rapidly, and the merits of both species are typically judged by flyfishers when the fish are in freshwater. Out in the saltwater, it's a whole different story.

When you mention saltwater and flyfishing in the same breath, most flyfishers will conjure up images of bonefish, tarpon, and other exotic saltwater species. However, with increasing regularity, flyfishers are looking toward saltwater that is closer to home. Flyfishers near the Gulf search the flats for redfish. Along the Atlantic seaboard they cast to bluefish and stripers. And along the West Coast, flyfishers chase stripers and salmon.

Although there are some long-time devotees of saltwater flyfishing in Alaska, only recently have many flyfishers tried it for the first time. These flyfishers are quickly finding out that Alaska's anadromous fish can frequently be intercepted while they are still in saltwater.

Salmon in Saltwater

From a sporting standpoint, saltwater is the most logical place to pursue Pacific salmon. Once salmon are in freshwater they stop feeding, and to get them to strike the fly-

Salmon in saltwater.

fisher has to rely on tendencies that are not as strong as the urge to eat. However, in saltwater, salmon are still actively looking for food.

In addition, when salmon are in freshwater they are constantly expending energy without replenishing it. Consequently, from the day they enter freshwater they are on the downhill slide from the peak of their fitness to their inevitable post-spawn death. Of course, all salmon that are in freshwater are not weak or near death. Anyone who has been miles from the ocean and has had a fly-hooked sockeye salmon rocket across the surface of the water in between leaps can attest to that. But just imagine this same fish while it is still in the salt before it has begun to deplete its energy reserves.

All of the salmon species found in Alaska can be caught by the flyfisher while they are still in saltwater, although some are easier to catch because of their habits. Pink salmon are typically the easiest to catch. Once they reach inshore waters, they usually travel very close to the surface. A flyfisher can often present a fly to them with a floating line, but getting a fly in front of the other four species of salmon is not always as easy as it is with pinks.

The majority of king salmon that are hooked on flies in saltwater are caught in southeast Alaska. It is here that there are resident kings in saltwater throughout the year. These feeder kings are immature fish that can be found at a wide range of depths, but they are frequently close enough to the surface to be taken with fly gear. Also, returning adults, here and in other parts of Alaska, typically begin to hug the shoreline and run at shallower depths as they approach their home rivers. This behavior results in the flyfisher getting a good shot at them.

Recently there has been a feeder king salmon fishery developing in south-central Alaska's Kachemak Bay during the winter and early spring. The climate in this area off the port of Homer can be quite mild during the winter, making for surprisingly bearable fishing conditions. Although I don't know any flyfishers who have tried it, it's probably just a matter of time before some of them fight off a bout of cabin fever by exploring the bay and seeing if there's a possibility of taking one of these saltwater kings on fly tackle.

Silver salmon are usually found in the top 30 feet of water, and like the pink salmon, they can also be taken very close to the surface. Silvers often spend a considerable amount of time milling around in the vicinity of a stream mouth. This habit translates into a great advantage for flyfishers when the stream mouth happens to be located inside a bay or cove. Not only will the fish be near the surface, but the flyfisher will probably be able to fish areas that have some protection from the wind and waves.

Sockeye salmon and chum salmon are more difficult to catch in saltwater than the previous three species. Sockeyes travel fast—as much as 30 miles per day—and they don't slow down at the mouth of a stream. Timing your fishing for them is extremely critical. Chum salmon run deep on their return journey, and even as they approach freshwater they may still be at depths of 50 feet or more.

I know there are flyfishers in Oregon and Washington who regularly take salmon at great depths, but if I can't find salmon fairly close to the surface, I will fish elsewhere for other fish. Fishing at depths of greater than 30 feet is not my idea of a good time. Besides, there is almost always some other kind of fishing available throughout the season in Alaska.

Saltwater Fishing for Other Species

Salmon are not the only fish that you can catch in the saltwater of Alaska. Sea-run Dolly Varden and cutthroat trout are quite common and sometimes easily caught. There are also species, such as rockfish, flounder, and even halibut, that can be taken on the fly. These last three species are not typically sought after in the world of flyfishing, but they can be fun to catch.

Protected coves and estuaries are the best bets for Dolly Varden and cutthroat trout. These fish are very localized and concentrated, and when you do find them, the action is usually fast and furious. Fly patterns and techniques for cutthroats are fully explained in the chapter on cutthroat trout, and they are the same methods needed for saltwater Dolly Varden fishing.

Rocky points and boulder-strewn shorelines are prime places to search for rockfish. Although it isn't common

Flyfishing for saltwater species.

knowledge, rockfish can be found in surprisingly shallow water during the summer. As the tide begins to go out, rockfish can be caught by casting to the downtide side of obstructions and points of land. Solid hits are often encountered while the fly is being retrieved against the current.

As you would expect, techniques for catching flounder and halibut on the fly rod are not well developed. I have only heard of a handful of flyfishers who venture out in pursuit of these two species. However, at times they are not difficult to catch, and sometimes while fishing river mouths, flounder can attack your fly with enough regularity to become a nuisance. Halibut come less often to the fly, but they have been taken under the same conditions as flounder. Halibut of 40 pounds and much larger have been taken from beaches in Alaska with conventional gear. If you hook into one that approaches this size while you are casting for salmon with your eight-weight ... good luck. The way these fish can head for the depths and hug the bottom doesn't give the flyfisher a good chance of ever seeing them.

Saltwater Fishing: Where and When

Alaska has thousands of miles of coastline, but the best flyfishing opportunities are found along the south-central and southeast coasts. The waters surrounding the Kenai Peninsula are frequented most often by anglers using conventional gear, but the flyfisher could do well here in selected spots. The eastern shore of Cook Inlet, especially in the vicinity of Deep Creek and the Anchor River, sees quite a bit of trolling traffic, but there is no reason why flyfishers couldn't pick up a few salmon if they didn't mind the crowds. Beach casting from the spit that protrudes from the town of Homer can also be productive for Dolly Varden.

The western shore of Cook Inlet has some good fishing, and it doesn't have the crowds. This is not a good place to make repeated crossings in a small craft because of the extreme tidal fluctuations. The water can get quite rough. The alternatives are to fly across the inlet with a small inflatable craft stowed away or to make reservations with a sport fishing operation located there. There is at least one that I know of that caters to flyfishers.

Another easily accessible spot on the Kenai Peninsula is Resurrection Bay. Here you can drive to the town of Seward and fish from shore at the head of the bay for silvers, pinks, and Dolly Varden. A small boat gives you access to more water, and a flyfisher using one will almost always be more successful.

Kodiak Island and its neighboring islands offer some splendid opportunities for the flyfisher. Here again, a boat allows the flyfisher to fish the waters more efficiently. There is a road system, though, and you could easily spend a couple of days driving to and from wadeable stretches of beach and casting for salmon and Dolly Varden.

The waters of Prince William Sound also offer great prospects for the flyfisher. All five salmon, Dolly Varden, and cutthroat trout (although they are localized) can be caught here. Of the three communities on Prince William Sound, Whittier, Valdez, and Cordova, the first can be reached by train, the second by car, and Cordova only by boat or plane. Once you arrive at one of these destinations, most of the fishing areas can be reached only by boat, making it a necessity in Prince William Sound.

Southeast Alaska is a gold mine for saltwater flyfishing. There are hundreds of miles of coastline where a flyfisher can cast to salmon, cutthroat trout, and Dolly Varden. Here again, a boat is necessary to get around and fish the water effectively.

Obviously, if you're interested in one particular species of salmon you will want to concentrate your fishing efforts to coincide with the return of that fish. Generally speaking, saltwater action begins to slow down considerably once the run has reached its half-way point. In many cases, a flyfisher keying in on salmon would want to try the saltwater as much as two weeks before the fish are expected to return to freshwater. One notable exception occurs in southeast Alaska. Here the opportunity to catch king salmon is extended because feeder kings are present throughout the year.

Sea-run Dolly Varden and cutthroat trout may be available as early as April in the Southeast, with good dates occurring as late as June as you move farther north. The warmest months of midsummer are the best to find rockfish, flounder, and the occasional halibut in water shallow enough for fly gear.

Fly Patterns for Saltwater

Some of my favorite baitfish patterns for use in saltwater are the Winnepesaukee Smelt, Zonkers in white and blue, and Thunder Creeks with a little Flashabou or Krystal Flash added to them. The Flash Fly with red or blue hackle has also been a good producer. These baitfish patterns, as well as other saltwater patterns, are typically tied in sizes 4 through 3/0, with 1/0 being the most common size.

For whatever reason, Woolly Buggers also work well in the salt. White, pink, and black are the colors I prefer. Other non-baitfish patterns that produce well are the Sparkle Shrimp and the Comets. The Sparkle Shrimp is best tied in pink, white, or a combination of the two. For Comets, I prefer to use gold, orange, or blue.

The Everglow Fly works particularly well in Alaska's saltwater. I first tried it in some of the protected waters of Prince William Sound, and it worked extremely well for silver salmon. Since that time I have used it with success for a variety of fish in many places. Many different colors will work, but my records indicate that a white body combined with a different-colored wing outperforms the solid colors. My standards for saltwater are chartreuse and white, blue and white, and red and white.

One August night when I was rowing a dinghy from shore to an anchored boat in Prince William Sound, I might have gained some insight into why the Everglow patterns are so effective. It was dark and every time the oars dipped into the water it seemed as if someone had just lit a multicolored sparkler. Thousands of tiny bioluminescent organisms emitted light with every disturbance of the oars. The Everglow Flies emit their own light, and somehow these two facts may be linked. I wish that I could say that this mini-light show prompted me to use Everglow Flies, but in actuality it didn't. I didn't put the two together until a later date.

Regardless of the species, finding fish and getting the fly in front of them in saltwater seems to be more important than the fly pattern being used. I have used many standard freshwater patterns in saltwater with good success. The Lambuth Candlefish and the Salmon Treat are the only two patterns that I currently use that were designed with saltwater use in mind.

If you intend to tie your own flies for saltwater, a word about hooks is in order. With freshwater flies the style of the hook is usually the fly tier's only concern, but for saltwater use the actual material that the hook is made of is equally important. Regular bronze-finished hooks will literally rust before your eyes when they are around saltwater.

Quite often fly tiers will automatically reach for a Mustad #34007 or a Mustad #3407 hook when they're tying flies for saltwater. These seem to be the most popular hooks. They do have many good applications, but they are not the only hooks available for saltwater use. Instead of restricting yourself to one style, take a good look around, because there are many other suitable corrosion-resistant hooks, including the Tiemco

Typical water for prospecting.

800S and 800B. These are not the only corrosion-resistant hooks, but they represent the styles that are available.

Tactics for Saltwater

Finding fish in saltwater is a prerequisite to catching them, and the most obvious markers of their whereabouts are the fish themselves. Once salmon get close enough to the freshwater river of their destination, they often give away their presence by jumping or rolling on the surface of the water. Often a careful approach is needed to get within casting distance of them at this time. If you can detect a pattern to their movement or figure out their direction of travel, it is best to give them a wide berth and head them off, positioning your boat in their lane of travel. Fishing from a stationary boat as the fish work toward you is very effective.

A flock of actively feeding birds means that baitfish are below, and salmon are probably not too far behind. In this situation try the same technique. Get in front of the moving school of fish and wait for them to come to you.

When there is no visible sign of surface activity, you'll have to do some blind prospecting. The best areas to search at this time are around points of land, kelp beds, and river mouths and their adjacent waters. Approach them carefully and present your fly as deep as possible for fish that may be suspended there.

Whenever I have fished the salt, I have found that erratic retrieves are the best producers. Everything from fast, six-inch strips to slow, foot-long pulls combined with unevenly spaced pauses is what I mean by an erratic retrieve. Falling into a monotonous retrieve sequence cast after cast seems to bore the fish as well as the angler.

Other than making your fly act as erratically as possible, the only other technique that I have observed that will be helpful to the flyfisher has to do with the relationship between the depth of the presentation and the speed of the retrieve. In almost all cases, the fastest retrieves work the best when the fly is close to the surface. In contrast, slow retrieves work better as you fish deeper.

Equipment for Saltwater

The rod that I would pick off of my rack if I was heading out to Alaska's saltwater would be a nine-and-a-half foot, eight-weight graphite. If I needed something heavier than the eight-weight, say for king salmon, I would skip the nine-weight and go straight to the 10-weight. When selecting a rod for saltwater fishing, think in terms of a tool that can punch a long line into the wind. Also keep in mind that you may want to throw shooting heads instead of full-length lines. For some flyfishers, this may mean selecting a different rod.

Anytime I consider purchasing a reel to match outfits eight-weight or heavier, I usually won't consider anything that is not suitable for saltwater. Whether it is in Alaska or along some coconut-ridden beach, all of my heavier outfits eventually find their way into saltwater. If you haven't already purchased a larger outfit but are thinking of doing so, I would highly recommend buying a top-of-the-line saltwater reel. Even if you never get to fish Alaska's saltwater, these reels perform wonderfully in our freshwater rivers and lakes.

Most of the reels that I'm referring to are listed as big game reels, and they are expensive. I have yet to find a good, cheap big game reel. The worst time to discover what I mean by a cheap reel is when a king salmon is still moving out after having already stripped out 50 yards of line. Compare

Flyfishing a tidal area.

the reels that are currently available and take a good look at their drag mechanisms, their weight, and their styling. Buy the one that you like the best and that you can't afford, as long as it will hold 150 to 200 yards of 20-pound backing with the appropriate weight line.

Shooting heads work well, and I do use them sometimes, but I prefer to cast full-length lines. However, shooting heads do provide a large measure of help when it comes time to balance your checkbook. Since I am often prone to buying reels that I can't afford, spare spools may be out of the question, at least right away. In these cases, a shooting head system is the only feasible alternative. For shooting heads, pick a floater, a mid-range sinker, and one with the fastest sink rate that you can find. I often add to my collection of shooting heads, and eventually I wind up with one of all of the various sink rates. I use all of them, but you'll be in good shape even if you have only a collection of the basic three.

As I said, I prefer to cast full-length lines when I can, and for saltwater my selection is fairly simple. I like to carry a weight-forward floater, an extra-fast, 10-foot sink-tip, and an extra-fast, 20-foot sink-tip line.

Leaders for fishing the salt in Alaska need not be anything special. Tippet strengths can range from six to 18 pounds, and their lengths can vary from three to nine feet. The longer leaders are best used with a floating line. Fast retrieves will keep your fly right up near the surface, and slower retrieves and weighted flies will let you fish effectively down to about six feet. With sinking lines, I use leaders of about four feet in length. For leaders of this length, I rarely bother with any kind of taper and instead use a straight piece of monofilament of the desired breaking strength.

Flyfishing in Alaska's saltwater is relatively new to all but a few flyfishers. As of yet, there are few standard fly patterns or flyfishing methods which have been developed specifically for the saltwater areas of Alaska. This then should make it very attractive to the adventurous flyfisher because of its challenges and the opportunities to experiment with new flies and techniques. Alaska is sometimes referred to as the last frontier, and on this premise, flyfishing Alaska's saltwater could be considered Alaska's last flyfishing frontier.

ALASKABOU

Chapter 16
Flies for Alaska

Having read the previous chapters, you should know
what fly patterns you need to have if you are targeting a particular species of fish in Alaska. It should also be obvious
by now that there is quite a bit of overlap. Take, for example, the ubiquitous Egg-Sucking Leech: it can be used for
just about any fish that swims in Alaska. Use this chapter
as a checklist in preparation for your trip to or your season
in Alaska. For a more detailed account of flies to use, see
my companion volume, *Flies For Alaska: A Guide to Buying & Tying*, available from Johnson Books, Boulder, Colorado, or your local fly shop.

How many of each pattern should you take? More than
enough. Alaska is not the best place to run out of flies,
because there's a very good chance that you won't be able
to replenish your supply once you start fishing. I don't ever
like to be without at least a dozen of any pattern that I
intend to use. Traveling with enough materials to tie flies

as you use them is an option, but if you have limited time to fish in Alaska, do you want to spend it tying flies?

Here's a good rule of thumb to follow. Decide on the number of flies that you can afford to buy or have the time to tie, and then double that number. It would be much better to return home with some extra flies than to have spend the last three days of your trip without the flies you want.

Most of the fly patterns I've mentioned will not be foreign to even the casual flyfisher. They're available through many fly shops and mail order companies, and they are also described in detail in the current crop of books that deal with fly patterns. The fly pattern appendix following this chapter describes a number of patterns that might not be familiar to you.

All the patterns are listed here in the full range of sizes that might be necessary if you were fishing the entire season in Alaska. Not all of the sizes will always be needed. This should be evident after reading previous chapters. A Flash Fly, for instance, could be tied as large as 1/0 or even 4/0 for king salmon, but obviously you wouldn't need a Flash Fly anywhere near that size if you were fishing for pink salmon.

I think that choice of hook style is best left up to individual taste. The hook is the basis for the fly, and under close scrutiny it may alter the look of the fly. In most cases I doubt that the fish will care. If you use a hook style you prefer, you will no doubt like the fly better than if you had used one you dislike, and as a result you will fish it with more confidence. I feel that this is more important than holding to exact details of the original pattern.

However, throughout this chapter and the fly pattern appendix, I have used Mustad and a few Tiemco hook numbers as a reference point. There are, of course, several other manufacturers that make hooks suitable for fly tying. Shop around and compare, there are lots of good hooks on the market.

On a similar note, please do not leave patterns at home because they are not mentioned in this book. Some fly patterns were developed and tied for purposes other than for those situations and species for which they are most effec-

Flies for Alaska.

tive. So, fish Alaska with a selection of flies that I have recommended, but also take along some of your favorites and some of those unnamed creations lurking around your tying table.

Single-Egg Flies

Single-egg flies are typically either a Glo-Bug or a chenille egg such as the Iliamna Pinkie. Both patterns have their advocates, but I prefer a chenille egg because it can be weighted. The Mustad #9174 or a similar hook is the standard, but there is no reason they cannot be tied on longer-shanked hooks. The following color selection is what you will need, whether you choose to use Iliamna Pinkies or Glo-Bugs.

I would be remiss here if I did not mention the use of plastic beads to imitate salmon eggs. It's not a new idea. In fact, some guides have been using orange-colored plastic beads as their ace-in-the-hole for many years while keeping them a secret. During the past couple of seasons, however, the general angling public has latched on to this deadly salmon egg imitation.

I'm not going to debate whether a plastic bead attached to a hook is a legitimate fly or not. It is, however, illegal to use a bead in waters that are classified in the sportfishing regulations as flyfishing-only. It is legal to use it elsewhere.

Iliamna Pinkie: Mustad #9174, sizes 6–8, 5x short, weighted; orange, pink, red, cream.
Glo-Bug: Mustad #9174, sizes 6–8, 5x short; orange, pink, red, cream.

Double-Egg Flies

The Two-Egg Sperm Fly and the Babine Special are the most well-known patterns in this category. The color of the chenille that is used for the bodies of these flies varies greatly, but it usually doesn't fall outside the spectrum of roe-simulating colors.

Recently some flyfishers have begun to tie grotesquely large single egg flies—essentially Glo-Bugs the size of golf balls—on hooks as large as 3/0. Typically they're referred to as Fat Freddies, and although they're not double-egg flies, because of their size it seemed more logical to include them here rather than with the single-egg flies. At times they're an excellent pattern to use for king salmon.

Babine Special: Mustad #36890, sizes 2-8, weighted; orange, red.
Battle Creek Special: Mustad #9672, sizes 2-8, 3x long, weighted.
Fat Freddy: Mustad #9174, sizes 3/0-2; orange, pink, red.
Two-Egg Sperm Fly: Mustad #36890, sizes 2-8.

Alevins

Alevin-imitating flies have been around for a long time, but it is not uncommon to find well-traveled flyfishers who have never heard of or seen an alevin pattern. Most patterns have a silver body, a tuft of orange yarn or marabou tied in at the throat position to imitate the egg sac, and small, bead-chain eyes. The patterns are spartan, but there is no need to add anything else to them.

Alevin: Mustad #9671, sizes 6-10, 2x long, weighted.
Egg & I: Mustad #9671, sizes 6-12, 2x long.
Fry Fly: Mustad #9671, sizes 6-10, 2x long.

Smolt Patterns

Smolt patterns are typically tied on long-shanked hooks in sizes 2 through 8. There are literally hundreds of patterns and styles, but the selection listed below is more than adequate.

Alaskan Smolt: Mustad #9575, sizes 2-6, 6x long, weighted.
Black-Nosed Dace: Mustad #9672, sizes 2-8, 3x long.
Blue Smolt: Mustad #9672 or #79580, sizes 2-8, 3x-4x long, weighted.
Coho Spectrum: Mustad #9575, sizes 2-6, 6x long, weighted.
Coronation: Mustad #79580, sizes 2-8, 4x long, weighted.
Squirrel Hair Smolt: Mustad #9672, sizes 2-8, 3x long.

Flesh Flies

Flesh flies come in two main forms, Woolly Buggers and Bunny Flies. The way to turn these two popular and simple patterns into flesh flies is to match the color of the pieces of salmon that are in the water. In most cases, spawned-out salmon have reddish-colored flesh but fungus and the blanching effect of the water tone it down. As a result, the predominant flesh colors are white, white and brown, and light pink and white.

There are times when these bulky Bunny Flies are just too much of a fly for very shallow and clear water. In these instances, savvy anglers use a fly that is nothing more than a wisp of teased out yarn tied to a hook. The yarn colors are the same as those described above for the other flesh flies.

Below is an assortment of flies you will want to have if you're matching the flesh.

Ginger Bunny Fly: Mustad #9672, sizes 2-4, 3x long, weighted.
White Bunny Fly: Mustad #9672, sizes 2-4, 3x long, weighted.

White Woolly Bugger: Mustad #9672, sizes 2-6, 3x long,
weighted.

Baitfish Patterns

There are small fish in Alaskan waters other than juvenile
salmon. They include whitefish, ciscoes, smelt, herring,
suckers, sticklebacks, and sculpins. Here again, the number
of existing patterns from which to choose is enormous. With
the following selection, you'll be able to match the local forage fish throughout Alaska.

Alaska Mary Ann: Mustad #9672, sizes 2-6, 3x long,
weighted and unweighted.
Arctic Minnow:Mustad #37187, size 2.
Black Ghost: Mustad #9672, #79580, or #9575, sizes 2-8,
3x-6x long.
Bumble Puppy: Mustad #36890, sizes 4/0-2.
Dahlberg Diver: Mustad #3366, sizes 1/0-2.
Gray Ghost: Mustad #9672, #79580, or #9575, sizes 2-8, 3x-
6x long.
Janssen Minnow: Mustad #9672, sizes 1-8, 3x long.
Lambuth Candlefish: Mustad #34007 or #3407, sizes 3/0-2,
weighted.
Lefty's Deceiver: Mustad #34007 or #3407, sizes 1/0-2;
white/blue or white/green.
Matuka Streamer: Mustad #9672, #79580, or #9575, sizes 2-
8, 3x-6x long, weighted; black or olive.
McNally Magnum: Mustad #34007 or #3407, sizes 1/0-2.
Mickey Finn: Mustad #9672, #79580, or #9575, sizes 2-8,
3x-4x long, weighted and unweighted.
Muddler Minnow: Mustad #9672, sizes 2-8, 3x long,
weighted and unweighted.
Olive Zonker: Mustad #79580, sizes 2-6, 4x long, weighted.
Thunder Creek: Mustad #9671, #9672, or #36620, sizes 4-
10, 2x-4x long; Black-Nosed Dace, Rainbow Trout
patterns.
Winnipesaukee Smelt: Mustad #9755, sizes 2-6, 6x long,
weighted.
Woolhead Sculpin: Mustad #9672, sizes 2-6, 3x long,
weighted.

Yellow Marabou: Mustad #9672, sizes 4-10, 3x long, weighted.

Nymphs

I think that if you're accomplished in nymphing techniques, you could visit Alaska from anywhere in the country and, with your own assortment of nymphs, be very successful. Most of the nymphs I use do not have names, because they're tied with the natural in mind, not a picture in a magazine or catalog. Here are standard patterns that I would recommend for Alaska.

A.P. Nymph: Mustad #9671, sizes 8-16, 2x long, weighted and unweighted; black, brown, olive.
Assam Dragon: Mustad #9671, size 4, 2x long, weighted.
Bitch Creek: Mustad #9672, sizes 2-10.
Brassie Nymph: Tiemco #3769, sizes 10-16.
Filoplume Damsel: Mustad #9671, sizes 10-12, 2x long, weighted.
Flash Body Nymph: Tiemco #200, sizes 8-14.
Flashabou Nymph: Mustad #9671, sizes 8-16, 2x long, weighted; black, brown, olive.
Gold-Ribbed Hare's Ear: Mustad #9671, sizes 8-16, 2x long, weighted.
Green Caddis Larva: Tiemco #200, sizes 12-18.
Marabou Girdle Bug: Mustad #9672, size 2-6.
Marabou Nymph: Mustad #9671, sizes 8-16, 2x long, weighted; black, brown, olive.
March Brown: Mustad #9671, sizes 8-12, 2x long, weighted.
Mosquito Larva: Mustad #94840, sizes 14-20.
Pheasant Tail Nymph: Mustad #9671, sizes 12-14, 2x long, weighted.
Woolly Worm: Mustad #9672, sizes 2-10, 3x long, weighted; black/grizzly.
Zug Bug: Mustad #9671, sizes 8-10, 2x long, weighted.

Woolly Buggers and Leeches

Leeches are found in Alaska, and Woolly Buggers are good flies to use to imitate them. Of course, Woolly Buggers are also good to use even if leeches are not present. The

Lake Leech listed below is also often referred to as a Marabou Leech.

Egg-Sucking Leech: Mustad #9672, sizes 2-6, 3x long, weighted.
Lake Leech: Mustad #9672, sizes 6-10, 3x long, weighted; black, brown, olive, purple.
Woolly Bugger: Mustad #9672, sizes 2-6, 3x long, weighted; black, brown, olive, orange, purple, white.

Scuds

Amphipods or scuds, as they are commonly called, are present in many Alaskan lakes. They range from a light, almost translucent color to bright orange and dark olive. In mixing the dubbing, the first color listed in the following color combinations is double the amount of the second color.

Scud: Mustad #3906, sizes 8-14; tan/pink, tan/orange, tan/olive.

Dry Flies

Alaskan game fish rarely become selective enough that the flyfisher needs to resort to a species-specific pattern when dry-fly fishing. General impressionistic patterns, usually referred to as attractors or searching patterns, are the best bets. The following assortment will take you through the season from start to finish throughout Alaska.

Adams: Mustad #94840, sizes 12-18.
Adams Parachute: Mustad #94840, sizes 12-18.
Black Gnat: Mustad #94840, sizes 12-18.
Black Gnat Parachute: Mustad #94840, sizes 12-18.
Blue-Winged Olive: Mustad #94840, sizes 14-18.
Bomber: Mustad #90240, size 4.
Disco Mouse: Mustad #90240, size 4.
Elk Hair Caddis: Mustad #94831, sizes 8-18.
Hornberg: Mustad #9671, sizes 6-16.
Humpy: Mustad #94840, sizes 8-18; black, orange, red, yellow.
Irresistible: Mustad #94840, sizes 10-14.

Flies for Alaska.

Katmai Slider: Mustad #9049, sizes 2-6.
Little Yellow Stone: Tiemco #2302, sizes 14-16.
Mosquito: Mustad #94840, sizes 12-18.
Mouserat: Mustad #37187, size 2.
Rio Grande Trude: Mustad #9672, sizes 8-14.
Steelhead Bee: Mustad #90240, sizes 6-8.
Wulff: Mustad #94840, sizes 6-14; gray, royal, white.

Steelhead Flies

Although these patterns are listed as steelhead flies, it does not preclude using them for other species or, for that matter, using other flies for steelhead.

Boss: Mustad #36890, sizes 1/0-6, weighted; black, chartreuse.
Bottlebrush: Mustad #36890, sizes 1/0-4.
Comet: Mustad #36890, sizes 1/0-6, weighted; gold, orange, silver.
Fall Favorite: Mustad #36890, sizes 2-6.
Frank's Fly: Mustad #36890, sizes 2-6.
Krystal Bullet: Mustad #36890, size 4, weighted; black, chartreuse, orange, pink, red.
Polar Shrimp: Mustad #36890, sizes 2-6, weighted.
Skunk: Mustad #36890, sizes 2-6, weighted; red butt, green butt.
Skykomish Sunrise: Mustad #36890, sizes 2-6, weighted.

Salmon Flies

There are many other flies that can be used for salmon, but here are nine that will get you through the Alaskan season, from king salmon to silvers. This may seem like a short list when you consider that there are five species of salmon in Alaska, but there are really 27 different flies listed here when you take into account the color variations.

Alaskabou: Mustad #34007 or #3407, sizes 3/0-4; hot pink/purple, chartreuse/white, orange/purple, white/pink.
Brassie: Mustad #36890, sizes 6-10.
Bunny Fly: Mustad #9672, sizes 2-4, 3x long, weighted; black, fuchsia, orange, pink, purple.
Deep Water Whistler: Mustad #34007 or #3407, sizes 3/0-1/0; orange/black, white/red.
Everglow Fly: Mustad #34007 or #3407, sizes 4/0-4, weighted; chartreuse, orange, orange/white, red.
Flash Fly: Mustad #34007 or #3407, sizes 3/0-4, weighted.
Maraflash Fly: Mustad #34007 or #3407, sizes 1/0-4, weighted; orange, purple, red, white.
Salmon Treat: Mustad #36890, sizes 3/0-6.

Sparkle Shrimp: Mustad #36890, sizes 1/0-4, weighted; hot
   pink, chartreuse, pink.
Wiggletail: Mustad #34007 or #3407, sizes 4/0-4, weighted;
   chartreuse, orange, pink.

Appendix A
Selected Fly Patterns

BUNNY FLY

Alaskabou, White/Pink
HOOK: Mustad #34007 or #3407, sizes 3/0-4
THREAD: Fluorescent red
TAIL: White marabou tied in at the midpoint of the shank, with a few strands of Krystal Flash or Flashabou
HACKLE: Pink
NOTE: Other popular color combinations are orange/purple, hot pink/purple, and chartreuse/white.

Alaska Mary Ann
HOOK: Mustad #9672, sizes 2-6, 3x long
THREAD: White
TAIL: Red hackle fibers
BODY: White chenille
RIBBING: Flat silver tinsel
THROAT: Red hackle fibers
WING: White calf tail with jungle cock shoulder
NOTE: This is the chenille-bodied version, and of course, the jungle cock is optional. If you are a traditionalist, go ¬head and use it. In that case you will also want to use the ¬ry floss for the body, red floss for the tail, polar bear hair ¬e wing, and black thread.

Alevin

HOOK:	Mustad #9671, sizes 6-10, 2x long
THREAD:	White
TAIL:	Unraveled pearl Mylar tubing
BODY:	Pearl Mylar tubing
THROAT:	Short orange or red marabou
EYES:	Small bead chain

Battle Creek Special

HOOK:	Mustad #9672, sizes 2-4, 3x long
THREAD:	White
TAIL:	White marabou
BODY:	Pink chenille
HACKLE:	White, palmered, with four wraps of orange hackle immediately behind the head

Blue Smolt

HOOK:	Mustad #9672 or #79580, sizes 2-8, 3x-4x long
THREAD:	White
TAIL:	Unraveled silver Mylar tubing
BODY:	Silver Mylar tubing
THROAT:	Red calf tail
WING:	Blue over white calf tail
TOPPING:	Mallard flank feather

Brassie

HOOK:	Mustad #36890, sizes 6-10
THREAD:	White
BODY:	Copper wire
WING:	White calf tail

Bumble Puppy

HOOK:	Mustad #36890, sizes 2-6
THREAD:	White
TAIL:	Red hackle fibers
BODY:	White chenille with red chenille egg sac
RIBBING:	Flat silver tinsel
WING:	White calf tail with jungle cock shoulder
HACKLE:	Teal flank feather

Bunny Fly

HOOK: Mustad #9672, sizes 2-6, 3x long
THREAD: White
TAIL: Short section of rabbit strip
BODY: Rabbit strip tied in at the rear and wound forward

NOTE: Ginger and white are used as flesh flies. It is also tied in purple, pink, black, and orange as an attractor pattern.

Coronation

HOOK: Mustad #79580, sizes 2-8, 4x long
THREAD: Black
TAIL: Unraveled silver Mylar tubing
BODY: Silver Mylar tubing
WING: Three layers of calf tail, blue on red on white

Dahlberg Diver

HOOK: Mustad #3360, sizes 1/0-4
THREAD: Red
TAIL: Gold Flashabou, black marabou, and two grizzly saddles
BODY: Rear half spun deer hair clipped flat on bottom and sides with top rounded; front half spun deer hair forming a 180-degree collar behind a bullet-shaped head

DISCO MOUSE

Disco Mouse
HOOK: Mustad #90240, sizes 2-6
THREAD: Black
TAIL: Silver Flashabou
BODY: Black thread
WING: Natural deer hair partially flared and clipped to form a head
NOTE: Dyed black deer hair is also used for a darker pattern.

Egg & I
HOOK: Mustad #9671, sizes 6-10, 2x long
THREAD: White
BODY: Silver tinsel with pink chenille formed into a ball on front quarter of hook
WING: Gray mallard flank

Egg-Sucking Leech
HOOK: Mustad #9672, sizes 2-8, 3x long
THREAD: White
TAIL: Purple marabou
BODY: Purple chenille with purple palmered hackle
HEAD: Pink chenille wrapped to form an egg shape

Everglow Fly, Chartreuse
HOOK: Mustad #34007 or #3407, sizes 4/0-4
THREAD: Chartreuse
UNDERBODY: White floss or chenille
BODY: Chartreuse Everglow tubing
UNDERWING: Chartreuse bucktail
WING: Chartreuse Everglow winging material
HACKLE: Chartreuse
NOTE: Other popular colors for the Everglow Fly are red, orange, and a white-bodied, orange-winged version.

Flash Fly
HOOK: Mustad #34007 or #3407, sizes 3/0-4
THREAD: Red
TAIL: Silver Flashabou
BODY: Silver Poly Flash

WING: Silver Flashabou
HACKLE: Red saddle hackle
NOTE: Different versions of the Flash Fly are created by changing the hackle and the thread color. The most popular colors are pink, orange, and purple.

Frank's Fly
HOOK: Mustad #36890, sizes 2-6
THREAD: Orange
BODY: Fluorescent orange chenille
WING: White calf tail
HACKLE: Orange, palmered

Fry Fly
HOOK: Mustad #9671, sizes 6-10, 2x long
THREAD: Black
TAIL: Sparse black calf tail
BODY: Gold tinsel
WING: Sparse black calf tail

Iliamna Pinkie (Pink Chenille Egg)
HOOK: Mustad #9174, sizes 6-8, 5x short
THREAD: Pink
BODY: Pink chenille wrapped to form a ball
NOTE: Chenille eggs can be tied in any color, but pink is by far the most effective.

Krystal Bullet, Red/Gold
HOOK: Mustad #36890, size 4
THREAD: Red
BODY: Chenille built up to form two distinct sections, with the rear largest
HACKLE: Gold Krystal Flash tied in at the front and folded back to be tied off between the two body segments
NOTE: There are hundreds of color combinations and none are standard. Go crazy.

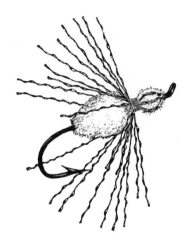

KRYSTAL BULLET

Lake Leech
HOOK: Mustad #9672, sizes 6-10, 3x long
THREAD: Black
TAIL: The tip of a full marabou feather
BODY: Remaining part of the tail feather twisted to form a single strand and then wrapped forward
NOTE: The number one color is purple with olive and brown running a close second. It's also tied in black.

Lambuth Candlefish
HOOK: Mustad #34007 or #3407, sizes 3/0-2
THREAD: Black
TAIL: Unraveled silver Mylar tubing
BODY: Silver Mylar tubing
WING: Three layers of calf tail, blue on red on white
TOPPING: Four strands of peacock sword
NOTE: This fly often has an eye painted on the head.

Maraflash Fly, Red
HOOK: Mustad #34007 or #3407, sizes 1/0-6
THREAD: Bright red

MAKAFLASH FLY

BODY: Poly Flash
WING: White marabou with a topping of silver
               Flashabou
NOTE: The color of the thread and marabou can also be
orange, white, or purple.

Mosquito Larva
HOOK: Mustad #94840, sizes 14-20
THREAD: Gray
BODY: Stripped peacock herl
HEAD: Two or three wraps of stripped peacock
               herl with five or six grizzly hackle fibers
               sticking straight out in front of the eye of
               the hook
NOTE: Larva is a misnomer; it's really a better imitation of
the pupa and is best fished as such.

Mouserat
HOOK: Mustad #37187, size 2
THREAD: Black
TAIL: Leather strip
BODY: Spun deer hair trimmed to shape
NOTE: The often added tail, ears, eyes, and monofilament
weed guard are optional.

Polar Shrimp
HOOK: Mustad #36890, sizes 2-6
THREAD: White
TAIL: Red hackle tips
BODY: Orange chenille
WING: White calf tail
HACKLE: Orange
NOTE: A very popular version of this is called the Hot Pink
Polar Shrimp. It is tied with hot pink chenille and hackle.

Sockeye Orange
HOOK: Mustad #36890, sizes 6-10
THREAD: Black
BODY: Flat silver tinsel
HACKLE: Orange
WING: Black calf tail or squirrel tail

Sparkle Shrimp, Hot Pink
HOOK: Mustad #36890, sizes 2-4
THREAD: Hot pink
TAIL AND
 SHELLBACK: Pearl Flashabou
BODY: Hot pink chenille

MOUSERAT

HACKLE: Hot pink, palmered

NOTE: The Sparkle Shrimp is also tied in chartreuse.

Wiggletail, Pink

HOOK: Mustad #34007 or #3407, sizes 4/0-4
THREAD: Pink
TAIL: Pink marabou
BODY: Pink chenille with palmered pink hackle
HACKLE: Unraveled Mylar tubing

NOTE: The Wiggletail is also tied in orange, chartreuse, and a pink-bodied, white-tailed version.

Appendix B
Alaskan State Records

Species	Lbs.	Oz.	Year	Location
Arctic char/				
Dolly Varden	19	12.5	1991	Noatak River
Arctic grayling	4	13	1981	Ugashik Narrows
Chum salmon	32	0	1985	Caamano Point
Cutthroat trout	8	6	1977	Wilson Lake
Halibut	440	0	1978	Icy Strait
King salmon	97	4	1985	Kenai River
Lake trout	47	0	1970	Clarence Lake
Northern pike	38	0	1978	Fish Creek
Pink salmon	12	9	1974	Moose River
Rainbow trout/				
steelhead	42	3	1970	Bell Island
Rockfish	26	0	1989	Kachemak Bay
Sheefish	53	0	1986	Pah River
Silver salmon	26	0	1976	Icy Straits
Sockeye salmon	16	0	1974	Kenai River
Whitefish	9	0	1989	Tozitna River

Appendix C
Common Names for Pacific Salmon

The names used for salmon are confusing, especially to flyfishers new to them. Throughout the book, the most common names for salmon among Alaskans have been used, but you may be more familiar with a different name. This listing should make it easier to be sure we're talking about the same fish.

The fives species of salmon found in Alaska and their common names:

Alaskan Salmon	Other Common Names
King salmon	chinook, tyee, springer, spring salmon, quinnat
Chum salmon	dog, calico
Sockeye salmon	red, kokanee (landlocked variety), blueback
Pink salmon	humpy, humpbacked
Silver salmon	coho

Index